P9-CQQ-193

SHANANDITTI

SHANANDITTI

THE LAST OF THE BEOTHUCKS

By Keith Winter

Copyright© Keith Winter, 1975

All rights reserved. No part of this book may be reproduced or transmitted in any form by any means without permission in writing from the publisher, except by a reviewer, who may quote brief passages in a review.

Canadian Shared Cataloguing in Publication Data

Winter, Keith John, 1935-
    Shananditti

    1. Shananditti, 1801-1829.   2. Beothuck
Indians.   I. Title.

E99.B4W55   970.3
ISBN 0-88894-086-6
Library of Congress number 75-24546

J.J. Douglas Ltd.
North Vancouver, British Columbia

Design by Heather Woodall
Typesetting by
Domino-Link Word and Data Processing
Printed and bound in Canada

All the names mentioned in this biography
are those of real people.
All the events are true.

For my parents, Jack and Alice Winter.

Any man's death diminshes me because
I am involved in mankind.

JOHN DONNE

Shananditti c. 1825

The Beothuck language was difficult to transcribe
with the English alphabet, and so Beothuck names
received many different spellings. Throughout the
years "Shawnawdithit," "Shanawdithit," etc.,
have been anglicized to the more pronounceable
Shananditti.

INTRODUCTION

The story of the life and death of Shananditti is symbolic of the tragic fate of the Beothuck Indians of Newfoundland. Shananditti was the last-known survivor, the last of a nation of about 50,000 people who lived in peace on the 42,734 square miles of the island of Newfoundland until it was discovered by European explorers in the 1500s. The Beothucks suffered more from their contact with the Europeans than did any other native people in North America: from disease, theft, massacres, starvation, and well-meaning governors' schemes that backfired and killed the very people they were intended to save.

Shananditti was an eyewitness to the catastrophes and terrible suffering during the last years of the Beothucks. She might have died unknown but for William Epps Cormack, a philanthropist who tried, though too late, to save the Beothucks from extinction. Cormack encouraged Shananditti to make drawings of the history and culture of her people; together they compiled a Beothuck vocabulary, and he wrote down what she was able to tell him. Unfortunately, only ten of Shananditti's sketches exist, and many of Cormack's notes have been lost. These fascinating glimpses and some scant archeological evidence are all that remain of the complex culture and obscure history of the Beothucks.

The early history of the Beothucks remains a mystery, although there is some evidence to suggest that they migrated from Asia across the frozen ice-bridge of the Bering Strait to the remote Aleutian Islands, south through the rugged wilderness of Alaska into the forests and mountains

1

of British Columbia, and then east over the two-mile-high barrier of the snow-capped Rocky Mountains, the vast fertile openness of the Great Plains and the numerous lakes and forests of the Canadian Shield, finally reaching the rocky wilds of Labrador. Archeological findings suggest that the Beothucks may have crossed the Strait of Belle Isle from Labrador to Newfoundland as long ago as ten centuries before the birth of Christ.

Why the Beothucks should want to cross over the strait into Newfoundland is anyone's guess. Perhaps hunting expeditions gradually grew into permanent residence. Perhaps the arrival of the Eskimos forced them to leave Labrador. There are traditions preserved by the present-day Indians of Labrador, the Nascaupi, that the Beothucks had already left before they arrived about a thousand years ago, although the Beothucks still returned occasionally to hunt seals. The Beothucks regarded the Nascaupi as their friends and equals, whereas they looked upon the Eskimos as their enemies and inferiors.

On an old sixteenth-century French chart, the Beothuck route between Labrador and Newfoundland is marked. It is called the "Chemin de Sauvage" (Trail of the Savages). In the *English Coast Pilot* of 1755 there is a place near Hawkes' Bay called "Passage de Savages." (See map page 145.)

The route across the strait touches Newfoundland at Savage Cove. From there, the old trail ran southward across a flat coastal bench towards Bonne Bay. The presence of the Long Range Mountains forced the migrating Beothucks along the coastal plain to where they found a natural route into the interior of Newfoundland.

The first permanent village was built at Norris Point on Bonne Bay, and this formed the eastern terminus for a gradual migration that in time covered the entire island of Newfoundland. It is possible today to trace the trail of Beothuck relics from Bonne Bay, across the height of land into the Humber Valley, east to Sandy Lake, and south to Grand Lake.

A second permanent village was built at the head of Grand Lake near the present town of Howley. This site was located on the main migration route of the caribou, an ideal spot for a village, and the Beothucks may have remained there for

2

centuries before the pressures of population forced them to spread eastward to the River Exploits, which eventually became the chief centre of their culture.

The River Exploits runs from the interior of Newfoundland to the sea at Notre Dame Bay. The Beothucks built two large villages on this river, one in the interior near Red Indian Lake, and one at the mouth of the river at Wigwam Point. These two villages corresponded to the seasonal migration of the Beothucks in their yearly quest for food. They hunted caribou in the interior during the fall and winter, then travelled about a hundred miles to the sea to hunt seal, birds, and whales during the summer. It was from this centre of population that the Beothucks slowly spread out in all directions and took possession of Newfoundland.

The Beothucks now enjoyed a rare privilege: a kingdom of their own, a safe country surrounded on all sides by the sea. With an abundance of food and no enemies, their cultural personality underwent a profound change. During the long arduous migration across Canada it had been necessary for them to be a tough, military people. Their bone breast ornaments suggest, in a stylized way, earlier forms of body armour, and their ceremonies of skull worship leave little doubt that they had once been head hunters—in fact, the only head hunters Canada has ever hosted. However, life in Newfoundland did not require combativeness, and the Beothucks gradually changed over hundreds of years into a gentle, peace-loving people fond of music and art.

In appearance the Beothucks were athletic and broad-chested, with "lithe active bodies." John Guy, who traded with the Beothucks in 1612, described them as "full-eyed." With jet black hair, regular features, and very even teeth to complement their large black eyes, the Beothucks were a handsome people.

About one physical feature of the Beothucks there has been disagreement: their height. The early fishermen often described them as a race of giants. A Mr. Richards claimed to have seen one at Notre Dame Bay who was seven feet tall, and a Mr. Watts of Harbour Grace reported a similar sighting. John Day, who was present when a group of men killed the last Beothuck chief, reported that the dead man measured six feet, seven and a half inches. Numerous fishermen have told how they found femur bones that were much larger than their own. Other reports, however, contradict these claims. Lieutenant John Buchan, who spent several hours in a Beothuck village at Red Indian Lake in 1811, made these observations:

Report has famed these Indians as being of gigantic stature. This is not the case, and must have originated from the bulkiness of their dress, and partly from misrepresentation. They are well formed and appear extremely healthy and athletic, and of medium structure, probably from five feet eight to five feet nine inches, and with one exception, black haired.

John Peyton, who sighted a number of Beothucks during his disastrous journey of 1819, confirmed that, with one exception, they were of average height. As with any nation, there were individuals who were very tall, but the more reliable reports indicate that the Beothucks were people of average stature. The exaggerated statements that they were giants were probably prompted by fear, or as James Howley suggests, "for the purpose of affording an excuse for the wanton destruction of such formidable enemies."

Along with their gentle dispositions, the Beothucks were a modest and generous people. They put a high value on children and on family life, and in many ways considered the sexes equal. There was very little sense of private ownership, except for clothing; they shared most goods communally, including fishing and hunting gear. They had a mellifluous language, loved to sing and dance, and made a habit of welcoming all strangers with feasts and friendship.

All these traits which made the Beothucks so attractive put them at a tremendous disadvantage when the Portuguese, Spanish, French, and English arrived on their shores in the 1500s. These profiteers from Europe had a fierce sense of private ownership which made the worst of them greedy, unscrupulous, and violent.

In the early days of European exploration the Beothucks welcomed these seafaring adventurers with feasts, songs, and dancing. This trust and friendship made them easy victims to the slave traders who lured whole families aboard their ships and sailed for Europe. At this time there was a brisk trade in dark-skinned slaves from Africa, but white-skinned slaves were preferred and brought higher prices. When the red ochre with which they stained their skin was washed off, the Beothucks were as fair-skinned as Europeans. It was this use of red ochre which prompted the early explorers to misname the Beothucks "Redskins" and "Red Indians."

The first slave expeditions began under a commission from the King of Portugal who proclaimed that the new island discovered by John Cabot was within the Portuguese sphere of influence and that all the property, including slaves, belonged to Portugal. In 1500 Gaspar de Corte-Real set out with three armed ships fitted to take on a cargo of slaves. Corte-Real and his ship disappeared at sea, but the other two ships reached Newfoundland. They traded with the Beothucks and filled the ships with a profitable cargo of furs. When they were ready to leave, they coaxed a large number of Beothucks on board, hoisted anchor, and set sail. As soon as they were out of sight of land, the unsuspecting Beothucks were seized, bound, and thrown into the hold along with the furs. Many died during the long voyage. Of the fifty-seven Beothucks who survived, two were presented as a gift to the King and the rest were sold on the slave market.

After a few years the Portuguese abandoned their slave expeditions, but the reason for this is not known. It is likely that the Beothucks soon died from various European diseases, just as they later died of tuberculosis when they lived near the settlers in Newfoundland.

The French and Spanish conducted slave expeditions during the next twenty years. Since the records of this inhuman traffic are sketchy, the number of Beothucks sold into slavery is unknown. In 1537 the transport of slaves from Newfoundland was brought to an end when the Pope publicly condemned it and threatened to excommunicate anyone who practised it.

In 1583 Sir Humphrey Gilbert formally annexed Newfoundland to England, and in 1610 the London and Bristol Company established a small settlement at Cupids on Conception Bay which was led by John Guy. Colonization was attempted also on the Avalon Peninsula, but for many years, British naval policy and British business interests actively opposed permanent settlement, or even allowing fishermen to winter in Newfoundland. The western fisheries were regarded as a hardy training ground for seamen who could be recruited into the navy, and English ports wanted to remain the centres for the profitable export trade in dried cod. Possession of the fisheries—Newfoundland's main prize—was identified with British maritime supremacy.

After the failure of the early colonies, authority was irregularly exercised by "fishing admirals." In 1729 an officer of the Royal Navy, Captain Henry Osborne, was appointed governor. His tenure was seasonal, as was that of his successors until 1817. In 1791 a civil court was instituted, and in 1792 a supreme court.

For many years the European population in Newfoundland was almost entirely seasonal. As late as 1684, there were only 120 permanent residents. Their numbers increased from 3,400 in 1754 to more than 12,000 by 1774: mainly Irish immigrants who worked for low wages in the cod fisheries. Food and supplies were shipped in from New England.

The fisheries in the late 1700s and early 1800s accounted for a steady increase in population; by 1804 it had reached 20,000. The peak year was 1814-15, when more than 11,000 immigrants arrived from southern Ireland to work in the shore fisheries. The prosperous deep-sea fishermen became resident merchants, buying dried cod, fish oil and sealskins for speculation abroad. Their headquarters was St. John's, which they transformed from a small fishing port to a distribution and financial centre.

The leading advocates of self-government on the island were William Carson, a Scottish physician, and Patrick Morris, an Irish merchant. In 1832 representative institutions were established with a bicameral legislature, which eventually became a single combined assembly.

The church played a dominant role in all Newfoundland communities. The population was divided into three main denominations: one-third were Roman Catholic, one-third Anglican, and one-quarter United Church members. Since one denomination frequently monopolized an entire community, the church was a strong social and political force.

The smallness and the scattering of the population influenced the Newfoundlander's character. Isolation from the outside world bred individuality and self-sufficiency. Customs changed slowly, and new ideas and technology were often resisted. On the other hand, Newfoundland people displayed humour and imagination in their folk songs and place names. The map of Newfoundland is dotted with poetic and imaginative names such as Heart's Delight, Come by Chance, Pushthrough, Little Tickle, and Ireland's Eye.

When European settlers had established a permanent foothold in Newfoundland, it became common practice to raid Beothuck villages to steal their stock of furs. These raids were unequalled in Canadian history for their brutality. Men were shot in the back as they ran away; women were butchered as they knelt, exposing their breasts to indicate their sex and begging for mercy, and the children were rounded up and their throats cut. Then the village was set afire.

Frequently the motive for these brutal murders was sheer sport. A group of fishermen at Notre Dame Bay tracked a party of Beothucks to their campsite and waited until they were asleep in their *mamateek*. Then they approached quietly and set fire to the dwelling of birch bark and pine poles, which was soon ablaze. As the Beothucks rushed out they were shot down. None escaped alive.

At Lower Lance Cove a number of fishermen from Old Perlican on Trinity Bay saw the smoke from a Beothuck camp. They approached cautiously and lay concealed all that night. At dawn the next morning they surprised the sleeping Beothucks with a burst of gunfire. Seven were killed; one of these was a man seven feet tall, and it took three shots to stop him. The fishermen decided to take him to Perlican for exhibition. There was no room in their boat for the huge body, so they tied a rope around his neck and towed him behind the boat. A strong wind arose and it was necessary to cut the corpse adrift.

Later the body washed ashore at a point of land near Lance Cove Head. It remained "festering in the sun till the autumnal gales and heavy seas dislodged it." All through the summer months, visitors came to view the huge body. The spot was afterwards named Savage Point.

The largest massacre occurred on a picturesque arm of land near Hant's Harbour. An armed party of fishermen surprised a village of four hundred Beothucks. They herded everyone together, including the children, and drove them to the end of the peninsula. There, crowded together on the last few yards of land, the terrified people stood helpless as the guns began to fire. Some knelt begging for mercy; others dove into the sea in a vain attempt to escape. The men and women were killed first. The children huddled together, crying, afraid, unable to comprehend the horror of mass execution. Then the fishermen moved in with knives and axes. They grabbed the children by the hair and cut their throats—they called it "killing the nits with the lice." The air was filled with the cries of the dying; the ground oozed with blood. The fishermen waded in and finished off the dying with their axes. Not one Beothuck escaped.

No one in the two hundred years of settlement in Newfoundland was punished for any of these crimes against the Beothucks.

As the vicious hunts and murders continued, the Beothucks were driven into hiding. Hunting and gathering food became more and more difficult; death by starvation and disease took an increasing toll on their diminishing numbers. By the end of the eighteenth century it was apparent that extinction was only a few decades away.

CHAPTER ONE

Shananditti was born on the rugged shore of a large lake in the interior of Newfoundland in 1801. In a clearing among the pines and the grey boulders at the northeast corner of the lake was the home of her parents. This was one of only four remaining Beothuck villages.

Her birth was an occasion to celebrate, as there were very few babies in that village on the lakeshore. By this time the Beothucks numbered less than two hundred people.

Shananditti's mother nursed her under a deerskin parka which was trimmed with beaver fur. The soft white skin of Shananditti contrasted sharply with the skin of her mother's hands, face and body, which were bright red from an application of red ochre. All the adults—old and young, male and female—that Shananditti saw in the village were bright red like her mother. The origin of this strange custom is lost in antiquity, but the reasons for its continued practice were mainly religious. As detailed later in the book, the Beothucks used red ochre in elaborate burial rites very similar to those of ancient Egypt in the second and third millenia B.C.

Shananditti lived with her mother, father, sister, cousin, and uncle in a large dwelling which they called a *mamateek*. (See on following page a sketch by Shananditti of the interior structure.) Long wooden poles were bound together by two octagonal hoops. These were covered with birch bark and dried deerskins. An opening at the top allowed smoke to escape from the fire built in a small pit in the centre. Earth was pushed up around the base to provide insulation, and protection from enemy arrows and guns.

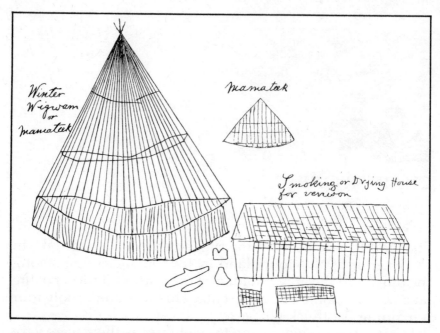

Winter Wigwam or mamateek

mamatek

Smoking or Drying House for venison

Shananditti's family slept each night in narrow trenches that were dug in the ground around the fire. These radiated from the centre like spokes in a wheel. In each two-foot-deep trench, lined with deerskins and beaver pelts, slept a member of the family in a sitting position, feet towards the fire.

As a young girl, Shananditti helped her mother and sister to gather berries and birds' eggs, but the bulk of the food gathering was done by her father. This was not an easy task, since all the Beothuck techniques of hunting and fishing were based on the participation of large numbers of men. For example, the Beothucks built huge wedge-shaped deer fences five to ten miles in length. Beaters drove the deer into the small enclosure at the apex, where it was an easy matter to kill them.

Now that the Beothucks were reduced drastically in population, they had to find new techniques of gathering food, and these were not always successful. Starvation became a constant threat. In the year that Shananditti was born there were more deaths from starvation than there were births.

In her youth Shananditti travelled with her parents on the last of the seasonal migrations for food. It was the centuries-

Deer fence (from Champlain) similar to that used by Beothucks.

old custom of the Beothucks to spend the winters in the interior of Newfoundland, and to journey each spring down the River Exploits to the seacoast at Notre Dame Bay. The hundred-mile journey down the River Exploits was made in oddly-shaped canoes. These were made of birch bark, and it is not known how their curious shape was derived. Models of these canoes have been found at a number of Beothuck burial sites.

Dimensions of a Beothuck canoe model.

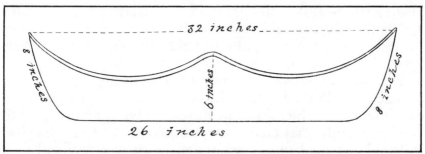

During the summer they hunted for seals and paddled to the offshore islands to collect the eggs of the Great Auk—a bird that could very well be taken as the emblem of the Beothucks, for it too is now extinct. The Beothucks are credited with the invention of powdered eggs. They collected the eggs of wild birds, boiled them by dropping hot rocks into birch bark containers of water, dried them in the sun, and later ground them into a fine powder. This highly nutritious powder was added to soups and stews.

A wealth of information comes from the drawings that Shananditti made as an adult. One of these, entitled "Different kinds of Animal food" (see illustration opposite) shows objects arranged in three horizontal rows. On the top are two odd shapes, labelled "Dried Salmon," presumably representing fish that have been cut, spread out, and tied with branches to hold them flat while they dry. In the middle are four oval shapes labelled "Dried meat"—either venison or seal meat. On the right are nine rows of small round objects joined together with a string. These are labelled "Lobsters tails dried."

On the second row is a gourd-shaped object labelled "A Deers Bladder filled with oil." This was undoubtedly seal oil, and it was probably used for heating, light, and cooking. The remainder of the row is filled with five rectangular shapes marked with dots and labelled "Pieces of Seals fat on the Skin."

The third row contains an interesting array of different shapes. The elongated, crossbarred object on the left is labelled "Bochmoot, or Seal skin Sledge full." It represents the entire skin of a seal, and the crossbars are an internal framework of wooden rods which made the skin hold its shape. Shananditti did not indicate what the Bochmoot was filled with. Seal skin sledges were also used by the European fishermen living in Newfoundland. They called them "nunny bags." When pulled in the direction of the hair's growth, they slid with great ease over the snow and ice.

The two oval shapes of different sizes in the third row are labelled "Seals Bladder filled with oil" and "Stomach of the Seal filled with the other intestines." It would be helpful to have more information on how the intestines were used. The sides of the next object are rolled or turned up, and it is

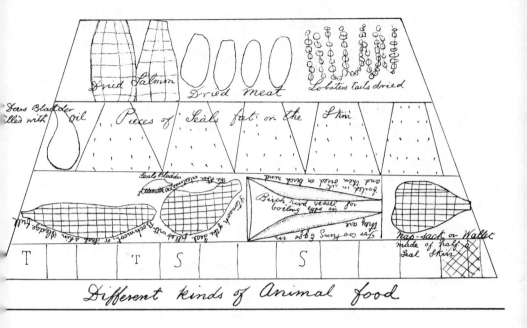

Dried Salmon

Dried meat

Lobsters tails dried

Deers Bladder filled with oil

Pieces of Seals fat on the Skin

Seal Bladder

Birch rind vessel for boiling eggs in

Nap-sack or Wallet made of half Seal Skin

T   T   S   S

Different kinds of Animal food

labelled "Birch rind vessel for boiling eggs in." It is stated that the eggs are boiled and dried on birch bark. The last object is fan-shaped, and it is labelled "Nap-sack or Wallet made of half a Seal Skin." Shananditti did not indicate its use, but it was probably for carrying oil or storing meat.

It is impossible to guess what the twelve rectangles at the base of the drawing represent. Since two are marked with a "T" and two with an "S," they must have meant something to Shananditti and the scholar who annotated them for her.

From Shananditti's detailed drawing of seafoods and wild animal foods it is clear that the Beothucks did not cultivate the land or domesticate livestock. They lived off the natural resources of the land and sea and they enjoyed a good selection of different foods.

During Shananditti's childhood it became increasingly more difficult, and often very dangerous, to obtain these foods. Several times she was forced to eat the inner bark of trees just to keep alive.

Shananditti soon learned that her life was in constant danger. This knowledge came to her in a painful episode that she never forgot. She carried the scars on her body for the rest of her life.

One morning she descended alone to the edge of the river to wash two pieces of venison. Suddenly a shot sounded from across the river. She felt a burning sensation in her leg and fell to the ground. On the opposite bank, she could see a white trapper reloading a long-barreled musket. Frantically she crawled up the bank. Another shot rang out, and blood gushed from her hand. She struggled on and finally reached the safety of the trees and made her way back to the village.

This unprovoked attack was not an isolated occurrence. There were many such shootings, and many trappers and fishermen boasted openly of their brutal exploits. Many kept running tallies of their kills. A few gained "reputations" for their large number of murders. There was Noel Boss, who killed ninety-nine Indians and was deeply disappointed because he could not make it an even hundred. There was a man named Rogers who killed over sixty.

But not all the white inhabitants of Newfoundland were bent on the destruction of the Beothucks. A few were genuinely concerned about the protection and preservation of their fellow man. In 1768, Sir Hugh Palliser, then governor of Newfoundland (he shares the credit with the Moravian Brethren for saving the Eskimos of Labrador from extinction) sent Lieutenant John Cartwright on a mission to contact the Beothucks.

As Cartwright journeyed up the River Exploits in search of Beothucks, it did not occur to him that his good intentions could be misunderstood. He did not realize that the Beothucks would see his armed party as a military invasion bent on destroying everyone in its path. It is hardly surprising that Lieutenant Cartwright did not get to shake hands with a single Beothuck.

After the failure of Cartwright's expedition, the government of Newfoundland let its Beothuck policy lapse for many years, until its interest in this persecuted minority was revived by Magistrate John Bland of Bonavista Bay. He advocated that a system of legal restraints be set up for the protection of the Beothucks, and he thought that the murder of a Beothuck should be viewed as a criminal offence. For twenty years John Bland wrote letters to various people in high places protesting the savage treatment that had gone unchecked:

It ought to be remembered that these savages have a natural right to this island, and every invasion of a natural right is a violation of the principle of justice. They have been progressively driven from South to North, and though their removal has been produced by a slow and silent operation, it has nevertheless had all the effect of violent compulsion. In proportion as their means of procuring subsistence became narrowed, their population must necessarily have decreased, and before the lapse of another century, the English nation, like the Spanish, may have affixed to its character the indelible reproach of having extirpated a whole race of people. The Spaniard, indeed, was stimulated by a passion which only great virtue can resist; and the inhumanities inflicted by some of our countrymen, on many occasions, upon the poor savages of Newfoundland, can hardly be conceived to originate in any other principle than a cruelty of disposition.

During the many years of correspondence, Magistrate Bland sent letters to several governors of Newfoundland, and out of this exchange sprang a bizarre idea: that a reward be offered for the capture of a living Beothuck. Surely this must be one of the most original ideas in the history of jurisprudence—a reward for the capture of innocent persons!

There were at least two proclamations issued, one by Governor John Holloway in 1807 offering a £50 reward, and one by Governor Sir Thomas Duckworth in 1810 offering a £100 reward. Apart from the monetary incentive, these documents acknowledged a spirit of brotherhood with the Beothucks, as seen in the opening remarks of John Holloway:

It having been represented to me that various acts of violence and inhuman cruelties, have been at different times, committed by some of the people employed as Furriers, or otherwise, upon the Indians, the original Inhabitants of this Island, residing in the interior parts thereof, contrary to every principle of religion and humanity, and in direct violation of His Majesty's mild and beneficial Instructions to me respecting this poor defenceless tribe, I hereby issue this my Proclamation, warning all persons whatsoever, from being guilty of acts of cruelty, violence, outrage and robbery against them, and if any Person or Persons shall be found after this Proclamation, to act in violation of it, they will be punished to the utmost rigor of the law, the same as if it had been committed against myself, or any other of His Majesty's Subjects.

It was reasoned that friendship could be established by lavishing the captive with gifts and indoctrinating him into the comforts and securities of "civilized life" in St. John's. Then the captive would be released and allowed to return to his people, where he would relate his gratitude to everyone he knew. In this way the legacy of fear built up by two hundred years of brutality and murder would be dispelled, and the Beothucks would be encouraged to form a lasting friendship which would lead to a lasting peace; this would stop the rapid decline in their population and save them from extinction.

When the reward was posted, it produced startling results. The humanitarian aims were lost in a stampede of greed. The trappers and fishermen did not care how many Beothucks they killed in their wild pursuit to capture one alive.

The intentions behind these proclamations were good, but the naivety of the whole scheme was appalling. In the sixteen years that the reward was offered, only five Beothucks were brought in to St. John's. These were all women. Three were so sick they died shortly after their capture; one was later murdered by her guide, and one had no family to return to. Of the many men, women and children killed by those in pursuit of the reward, no record was kept.

Clearly a new approach was needed, and in 1808 Governor Holloway came up with an ingenious and equally futile plan. He commissioned an oil painting which showed "an officer of the Royal Navy in full dress shaking hands with an Indian Chief, and pointing to a party of seamen behind him who were laying some bales of goods at the feet of the Chief. Behind the latter were some male and female Indians presenting furs to the Officers. Further to the left were seen a European and an Indian mother looking with delight at their respective children of the same size, who were embracing one another. In the opposite corner a British tar was courting, in his way, an Indian Beauty."

The governor took great pains with this large canvas and entertained high hopes for its success. He had it painted in England and carried by coach to Portsmouth, and it accompanied the governor on a ship across the Atlantic. Then it was loaded on another ship at St. John's and sent to the Bay of Exploits. Lieutenant Spratt and a party of men carried it up the River Exploits and left it with a bundle of gifts at a spot frequented by the Beothucks. No one appeared to claim the gifts, or to peer at the painting. Some time later, Lieutenant Spratt returned and carried the painting back to St. John's, where it was hung in the Court House.

Before leaving Newfoundland in 1809, Governor Holloway made one more attempt to establish friendly contact with the Beothucks. He hired William Cull and several other men to make a journey into the interior to meet the Beothucks and to offer them gifts in friendship. The governor's scheme failed, and this is hardly surprising. William Cull and the entire party of fishermen and trappers had been killing Beothucks for sport for years. They were recognized murderers. It is hard to believe that the governor did not know this. Did he expect them to kill with one hand and to offer charity with the other?

There is evidence that William Cull and his party made no effort to do what they had promised. They simply kept the gifts and made no attempt to deliver them. Governor Holloway expressed his suspicions about an earlier and similar party to Viscount Castlereagh: "I suspect that the parties hitherto employed on this Service have purloined the Articles intended to have been given to the Indians and have claimed remuneration for pretended endeavours of effecting a social intercourse and friendship, which they have never attempted."

CHAPTER TWO

During the winter of 1811 Shananditti was an eyewitness to a daring and courageous attempt to make friendly contact with her people. A military expedition led by Lieutenant David Buchan made a valiant effort to save the Beothucks from extinction.

Lieutenant Buchan was sent by Governor Sir Thomas Duckworth to make friendly contact with the Beothucks and to persuade them to open trade with the "civilized world." A large supply of knives, beads, blankets, scissors, hatchets, mirrors, pots, fishing lines, hooks, needles, thread, awls, hammers, nails, spoons, teapots, traps, files, hats, and socks was to be given to the Beothucks as an expression of good will. It was naively believed that this would restore their trust and bring prosperity to their declining numbers.

Although Lieutenant David Buchan repeated all the earlier mistakes of Cartwright, he tried harder, suffered more, and adventured farther than did any preceding expedition.

With an armed party, he sailed from St. John's aboard the armed schooner *Adonis* for the Bay of Exploits. The ship carried a large quantity of gifts as well as weapons and supplies. He arrived at the ancient habitat of the Beothucks in August and anchored in the bay. The next two months were spent waiting patiently for the Beothucks, but none appeared. He decided to wait until winter and travel up the river on the ice with his men pulling their equipment and the gifts on sleds. Here is Buchan's account of this attempt:

SATURDAY, JANUARY 12TH, 1811. On the eve of this date my arrangements were closed, and every necessary preparation made to advance into the interior, for the purpose of endeavouring to accomplish the grand object of your orders, relative to the Native Indians of this Island. For this service I employed William Cull and Mathew Hughster as guides, attended by twenty three men and a boy of the crew of his Majesty's schooner, and Thomas Taylor, a man in Mr. Miller's employ, and well acquainted with this part of the country.

The provisions, arms and other requisite articles, together with presents for the Indians, were packed on twelve sledges, and consisted of as follows: bread 850 lbs., sugar 100 lbs., cocoa 34 lbs., pork 660 lbs., salt fish 30 lbs., spirits 60 gals., equal to 480 lbs., rice 30 lbs., tea 6 lbs., tare of casks and packages 500 lbs., ships muskets, seven; fowling pieces, three; pistols, six; cutlasses, six; with cartouch boxes and ammunition equal to 270 lbs.; ten axes, and culinary utensils, forty pounds. Presents for the Indians; blankets 30, woollen wrappers nine; flannel shirts eighteen; hatchets twenty-six; tin pots, ten; with beads, thread, knives, needles, and other trifles, equal to 180 lbs. The sledges with their lashings and drag ropes are estimated at 240 lbs. One lower studding sail and painted canvas covers for the sledges, 120 lbs., spare snow shoes, Buskins, vamps, cuffs, and 28 knapsacks, eighty pounds; making independent of a small quantity of baggage allowed to each individual 3,600 pounds.

JAN. 13TH. WIND NW., BLOWING STRONG. At 7 A.M. commenced our march; in crossing the arm from the schooner to Little Peter's Point which is two miles, we found it extremely cold, and the snow drifting, and the sledges heavy to haul from the sloppiness of the ice, but having rounded the Point we became sheltered from the wind until reaching Wigwam Point, which is two miles further up on the north side; here the river turns to the northward; a mile further on is Mr. Miller's upper salmon station; the winter crew have their house on the south shore. 3 P.M., having reached the remains of a house occupied by Wm. Cull last winter we put up for the night, our distance made good being but eight miles in as many hours travelling. The night proved so intensely cold, with light snow at times, that none of our party could refresh themselves with sleep.

JAN. 14TH. WIND NW., WITH SHARP PIERCING WEATHER. Renewed our journey with the dawn, not sorry to leave a place in which we had passed so intolerable a night. Having proceeded on two miles, we came to the Nutt Islands, four in number, situated in the middle of that river; a mile above these is the first rattle or small waterfall, as far as the eye could discern up the river, nothing but ridgy ice appeared, its aspect almost precluded the possibility of conveying the sledges along; but determined to surmount all practicable difficulties, I proceeded on with the guides to choose among the hollows those most favorable. 3 P.M. put up on the north side, and fenced round the fireplace for shelter. This day's laborious journey I computed to be seven miles; the crew, from excessive fatigue, and the night somewhat milder than last, enjoyed some sleep. Left a cask with bread, pork, cocoa and sugar for two days, to be used on our return.

JAN. 15TH. BLOWING FRESH FROM WNW. TO NNW. WITH SNOW AT TIMES; the river winding from W. to NW. At 3 P.M. stopped on the north bank for the night, one mile above the Rattling Brook, which empties itself into this river. On the south side, on the western bank of its entrance, we discovered a canoe which I observed to be one that belonged to the Canadians who had resided at Wigwam Point. This day's journey exhibited the same difficulties as yesterday, having frequently to advance a party to cut and level, in some degree, the ridges of ice to admit the sledges to pass from one gulf to another, and to fill up the hollows to prevent them from being precipitated so violently as to be dashed to pieces; but notwithstanding the utmost care, the lashings from the constant friction, frequently gave way; and in the evening, most of the sledges had to undergo some repair and fresh packing. Fenced the fire-place in; at supper the people appeared in good spirits; the weather milder; fatigue produced a tolerable night's rest. The day's distance is estimated to be seven miles.

JAN. 16TH. STRONG BREEZES FROM NNW. WITH SHARP FROST. Began our journey with the day. Several of the sledges gave way, which delayed us a considerable time. At 11 A.M. discovered two old wigwams on the north bank of the river; although they did not appear to have been lately inhabited, yet there were some indications of the natives having been here this fall. 2 P.M. Having reached the lower extremity of the great waterfall, we put up on the north side. While the party were preparing a fire and fence, I proceeded on, with Cull and Taylor, in search of an Indian path through which they convey their canoes into the river above the overfall. Taylor, not having been here for many years, had lost all recollection where to find it; after a tedious search we fortunately fell in with it; there were evident signs of their having passed this way lately, but not apparently in any great number. Evening advancing, we retraced our steps, and reached our fire-place with the close of day. The night proved more mild than any hitherto, and our rest proportionally better. Here I left bread, pork, cocoa and sugar for two days, and four gallons of rum.

JAN. 17TH. SOUTH-WESTERLY WINDS, WITH SLEET, AND RAW COLD WEATHER. Began this day's route by conducting the sledges in a winding direction amongst high rocks, forming the lower extremity of the waterfall; having proceeded half a mile, we had to unload and parbuckle the casks over the perpendicular neck of land, which projecting into the rapid prevented the ice attaching to its edge, having reloaded on the opposite side, and turned the margin of coves for a third of a mile, we arrived at the foot of a steep bank, where commences the Indian path; here it was also necessary to unload. Leaving the party to convey the things up the bank, I went on with Cull and Taylor, to discover the further end of the path; having come to a marsh, it was with difficulty we again traced it; at length we reached the river above the overfall, its whole extent being one mile and a quarter; having gone on two miles beyond this, we returned. At noon, the wind having veered to the S.E. it came on to rain heavily; sent a division on to the further end of the path to prepare a fire, etc. 3 P.M. All the light baggage and arms being conveyed to the fire-place, the sledges were left for the night halfway in the path, so that after eight hours fatigue, we had got little farther than one mile and a half. It continued to rain hard until 9 P.M. when the wind shifted round to the westward, and cleared up, the crew dried their clothes, and retired to rest.

JAN. 18TH. WIND WNW. AND COLD WEATHER. Leaving the party to bring on the sledges to the Indian Dock, and to repack them, I and the guides having advanced a mile, it was found requisite to cut a path of a hundred yards to pass over a point which the sledges could not round for want of sufficient ice being attached to it.

10 A.M. We now rounded a bay leaving several islands on our left; the travelling pretty good, except in some places where the ice was very narrow, and water oozing over the surface; most of us got wet feet. 2:30 P.M. Put up in a cave on the north shore as we should have been unable to reach before dark another place where good fire-wood was to be found; here the river forms a bay on either side, leaving between them a space of nearly one mile and a half, in which stood several islands, from the overfall up to these, the

22

river in its centre was open. Having given directions for a fireplace to be fenced in, and the sledges requiring to be repaired, Cull and myself went on two miles to Rushy Pond Marsh, where he had been last winter; two wigwams were removed which he stated to have been there. The trees leading from the river to the marsh were marked, and in some places a fence-work thrown up; the bushes in a particular line of direction through a long extent of marsh had wisps of birch bark suspended to them by salmon twine, so placed as to direct the deer down to the river; we killed two partridges and returned to the party by an inland route; we reckon the distance from Indian Dock to this resting-place to be six miles.

JAN. 19TH. WESTERLY WIND AND MODERATE, BUT VERY COLD. Most of this day's travelling smooth, whith dead snow, the sledges consequently hauled heavy; having winded for two miles amongst rough ice to gain a green wood on the south shore, that on the north being entirely burnt down, we put up at 4 P.M. A little way on the bank of a brook, where we deposited a cask with bread, pork, cocoa and sugar for two days consumption. In all this day's route the river was entirely frozen over; we passed several islands; saw a fox and killed a partridge, estimated distance ten miles; rested tolerably during night.

SUNDAY, JAN. 20TH. WIND WNW. AND COLD. Renewed our journey with the first appearance of day; at first setting out, the sledges, in passing over a mile of sharp pointed ice, broke two of them; repairing and packing delayed some time. At noon the sun shone forth, the weather warm, and a fine clear sky.
4 P.M. Halted on an island situated two miles above Badger Bay Brook, which fall into this. On the north side it appears wide, with an island in its entrance, and the remains of a wigwam on it. From this brook upwards, as also on the opposite side of the river, are fences of several miles, and one likewise extended in a westerly direction, through the island on which we halted, and is calculated to be twelve miles from the last sleeping place, and twenty miles from the Indian Dock: Hodge's Hills bearing from this ESE.

JAN. 21ST. WIND WESTERLY, WITH BLEAK WEATHER. At dawn proceeded on. At noon several difficulties presented themselves in crossing a tract of shelvy ice, intersected with deep and wide rents, occasioned by a waterfall: the sledges were, however, got over them, as also some steps on the north bank. Having ascended the waterfall, found the river open and faced with ice sufficient on the edge of its banks to admit the sledges. At 4:30 P.M. up for the night, and fenced in a fire-place. This day's distance is estimated at eleven miles, allowing seven from the island on which we slept last night up to the overfall, and from thence to this.

From the waterfall upwards, on either side of the river where the natural bank would have been insufficient, fences were thrown up to prevent the deer from landing, after taking to the water, by gaps left open for that purpose. Repacked the sledges, two of them being unfit to go on farther, deposited a cask with bread, pork, cocoa, and sugar, for two days. The party slept well.

JAN. 22ND. SW. WINDS WITH MILD HAZY WEATHER. Having advanced two miles, on the south side, stood a store-house: Wm. Cull stated that no such building was there last winter; it appeared newly erected and its form circular, and covered round with deer skins, and some carcases left a little way from it; two poles were stuck close to the water, as if canoes had lately been there. Four miles from this, passed an Island, and rounded a bay, two miles beyond its western extremity, on a projecting rock, were placed several stag's horns. Wm. Cull now informed me that it was at this place he had examined the store-houses (mentioned in his narrative), but now no vestige of them appeared: there was, however, ample room cleared of wood for such a building described to have stood, and at a few hundred yards off was the frame of a wigwam still standing; close to this was a deerskin hanging to a tree, and further on a trope with the name of "Rousell"; the Rousells live in Sops Arm and in New Bay. On the south bank, a little lower down, also stood the remains of a wigwam, close to which Cull pointed out the other store to have been; a quarter of a mile below on the same side, a river, considerable in appearance, emptied itself into this; directly against its entrance stands an Island well wooded. We continued on four miles, and then the party stopped for the night. Cull accompanied me two miles farther and we returned at Sunset. During this day's journey, at intervals, we could discern a track which bore the appearance of a man's foot going upwards. One of the sledges fell into the water, but it fortunately happened to be a shoal part; nothing was lost. Our distance made good today we allow to be twelve miles, and the river open from the last overfall with scarcely enough ice attached to the bank to admit the sledges to pass on, and there are banks and fences in such places as the natives find necessary to obstruct the landing of the deer, some of these extending two or three miles, others striking inland. Divided the party into three watches, those on guard, under arms during the night.

JAN. 23RD. WIND WESTERLY, WILD COLD WEATHER. At daylight renewed our journey: the river now shoaled and ran rapidly, I wished to have forded it, conceiving that the Indians inhabited the other side, but found it impracticable. At 10 A.M., having advanced six miles, and seeing the impossibility of proceeding farther with the sledges, I divided the party, leaving one half to take care of the stores, whilst the other accompanied me, and taking with us four days' provisions, we renewed our route, the river now winded more northerly. Having proceeded on about four miles, we observed on the south side a path in the snow where a canoe had evidently been hauled across to get above a rattle, this being the only sure indication that we had discovered of their having passed upwards from the store on the south side. The river narrowed, ran irregular and diminished in depth very considerably. Having passed several small rivers on this side, we came abreast of an island, opposite to which, on the south side, was a path in the snow, from the water, ascending a bank where the trees were very recently cut, clearly evincing the residence of the natives to be at no great distance; but it being impossible to ford the river at this place, we continued on, but had not gone more than a mile, when turning a point, an expansive view opened out, and we saw before us an immense lake extending nearly in a NE. and SW. direction, its surface a smooth sheet of ice. We saw tracks but could not be certain whether of deer or men. We had lost for some miles the trace seen yesterday. On approaching the pond or lake we discovered on its NW. side two bodies in motion, but were uncertain if men or quadrupeds, it being nearly three o'clock. I drew the party suddenly into the wood to prevent discovery, and directed them to prepare a place for the night. I went on to reconnoitre. Having skirted along the woods for nearly two miles, we posted ourselves in a position to observe their motions; one gained ground considerably on the other: we continued in doubt of their being men until just before loosing sight of them in the twilight; it was discernible that the hindermost dragged a sledge. Nothing more could be done until morning, as it would have been impossible to have found their track in the dark; observing, on our return, a shovel in a bank of snow, we found that venison had been dug out, we however, found a fine heart and liver; this made a good supper for the party, whom we did not rejoin till dark. One third of the party were successively under arms during the night, which proved excessively cold and restless to all.

JAN. 24TH. WIND NE. AND INTENSELY COLD. Having refreshed

ourselves with breakfast and a dram to each at 4 A.M. commenced our march along the east shore with the utmost silence; beyond the point from whence I had the last view of the two natives, we fell in with a quantity of venison in carcases and quarters, close to which was a path into the wood. Conjecturing that the Indians' habitations were here, we advanced in, but found it to be an old one; the party complained much of the cold, and occasionally sheltered themselves under the lee of the points. It at length became necessary to cross the pond in order to gain the track of their sledge; this exposed us entirely to the bitterness of the morning; all complained of excessive cold. With the first glimpse of morn, we reached the wished-for track; this led us along the western shore to the NE., up to a point, on which stood an old wigwam; then struck athwart for the shore we had left. As the day opened it was requisite to push forth with celerity to prevent being seen, and to surprise the natives whilst asleep. Canoes were soon descried, and shortly wigwams two close to each other and the third a hundred yards from the former. Having examined the arms, I charged my men to be prompt in executing such orders as might be given, at the same time strictly charging them to avoid every impropriety, and to be especially guarded in their behavior towards women. The bank was now ascended with great alacrity and silence, the party being formed into three divisions; the wigwams were at once secured. On calling to the people within, and receiving no answer, the skins which covered the entrance were then removed, and we beheld groups of men, women and children lying in the utmost consternation; they remained absolutely for some minutes without motion or utterance. My first object was now to remove their fears, and inspire confidence in us, which was soon accomplished by our shaking hands, and showing every friendly disposition. The woman embraced me for my attentions to their children; from the utmost state of alarm they soon became curious, and examined our dress with great attention and surprise. They kindled a fire and presented us with venison steaks, and fat run into a solid cake, which they used with meat. Everything promised the utmost cordiality; knives, handkerchiefs, and other little articles were presented to them, and in return they offered us skins. I had to regret our utter ignorance of their language, [that] the presents [were] at a distance of at least twelve miles, occasioned me much embarrassment; I used every endeavour to make them understand my great desire that some of them should accompany us to the place where our baggage was, and assist bringing up such things as we wore, which at last they seemed perfectly to comprehend. Three hours and a half having

26

been employed in conciliatory endeavours, and every appearance of the greatest amity subsisting between us; and considering a longer tarry useless, without the means of convincing them farther of our friendship, giving them to understand that we were going, and indicating our intentions to return, four of them signified that they would accompany us. James Butler, corporal, and Thomas Bouthland, private of marines, observing this, requested to be left behind in order to repair their snow shoes; and such was the confidence placed by my people in the natives that most of the party wished to be the individuals to remain among them, I was induced to comply with the first request from a motive of showing the natives a mutual confidence, and cautioning them to observe the utmost regularity of conduct, at 10 A.M., having myself again shook hands with all the natives, and expressed, in the best way I could, my intentions to be with them in the morning, we set out. They expressed satisfaction by signs on seeing that two of us were going to remain with them, and we left them accompanied by four of them. On reaching the river head, two of the Indians struck into our last night's fire place. One of these I considered to be their chief; finding nothing there for him, he directed two of them to continue on with us. These went with cheerfulness, though at times they seemed to mistrust us. Parts of the river having no ice it was difficult to get along the banks occasioning at times a consid-erable distance between me and the hindermost Indian. Being under the necessity of going single, in turning a point one of the Indians, having loitered behind, took the opportunity and set off with great speed, calling out to his comrade to follow. Previous precautions prevented his being fired at. This incident was truly unfortunate as we were nearly in sight of our fire place. It is not improbable but he might have seen the smoke, and this caused his flight, or [it was] actuated by his own fears, as no action of my people could have given rise to his conduct. He had however, evidently some suspicions, as he had frequently come and looked eagerly in my face, as if to read my intentions. I had been most scrupulous in avoiding every action and gesture that might cause the least distrust. In order to try the disposition of the remaining Indian, he was made to understand that he was at liberty to go if he chose, but he showed no wish of this kind. At 3 P.M. we joined the rest of our party, when the Indian started at seeing so many more men; but this was of momentary duration, for he soon became pleased with all he saw; I made him a few presents and showed the articles which were to be taken up for his countrymen consisting of blankets, woolen wrappers, and shirts, bead, hatchets, knives and tin pots, thread, needles, and fish hooks, with which he appeared much satisfied, and regaled himself with tea and broiled venison, for we brought down two haunches with us in the evening. A pair of trousers and vamps, being made out of a blanket, and a flannel shirt being presented to him he put them on with sensible pleasure, carefully avoiding any indecency; being under no restraint, he occasionally went out, and he expressed a strong desire for canvass, pointing to a studding sail which covered us in on one side. He laid by me during the night. Still my mind was somewhat disturbed, for it occurred to me that the natives on the return of their comrade who deserted us, might be induced from his misrepresentation dictated by fear to quit the wigwams and observe our motions, but I was willing to suppress any fear for the safety of our men, judging that they would not commit any violence, until they should see if we returned and brought their companion; I was moreover satisfied that the conduct of our men would be such as not to give occasion to any animosity, and in the event of their being removed they would see the impossibility of safety in any attempt to escape.

FRIDAY THE 25TH OF JAN. WIND NNE. AND BOISTEROUS WITH SLEET. At 7 A.M. set out, leaving only eight of the party behind. On coming up to the river head, we observed the tracks of three men crossing the pond in a direction for the other side of the river. The violence of the wind with the sleet and drift snow rendered it laborious to get on, and so thick was it at times that all the party could not be discerned, although at no great distance from each other. When within half a mile of the wigwams, the Indian who walked sometimes on before, at others by my side, pointed out an arrow sticking in the ice; we also perceived a recent track of a sledge. At 2 P.M. we arrived at the wigwams, when my apprehensions were unfortunately verified; they were left in confusion, nothing of consequence remaining in them but some deer skins. We found a quantity of venison packs conveyed a little way off, and deposited in the snow; a path extended into the wood, but to no distance. Perceiving no mark of violence to have been committed, I hoped that my former conjectures would be realized, and that all would yet be well. The actions of the Indian however, were indicative of extreme perplexity and are not describable. Having directed the fire to be removed from the wigwam we were now in to one more commodious; one of the people taking up a brand for that purpose, he appeared terrified to the last degree, and used his utmost endeavour to prevent its being carried out. He either apprehended that we were going to destroy the wigwams and canoes (of which latter there were six) or that a fire was going to be kindled for his destruction. For sometime he anxiously peeped through the crevices to see what was doing, for he was not at liberty. Perplexed how to act, and evening drawing on, anxiety for the two marines determined me to let the Indian go, trusting that his appearance and recital of our behaviour would not only be the means of our mens' liberation, but also that the natives would return with a favourable impression. After giving him several things, I showed a wish that his party should return, and by signs intimated not to hurt our people. He smiled significantly, but he would not leave us. He put the wigwam in order, and several times looked to the west side of the pond and pointed. Each wigwam had a quantity of deers' leg bones ranged on poles (in all three hundred). Having used the marrow of some of these opposite that we occupied, the Indian replaced them with an equal number of other signifying that these were his; he pointed out a staff and showed that it belonged to the person that wore the high cap, the same that I had taken to be the chief; the length of this badge was nearly six feet, and two inches at the head, tapering to the end, terminating in not more than three quarters of an inch; it presented four plain equal sides, except at the upper end, where it resembled three rims one over the other, and the whole stained red. The day having closed in, it blew very hard, with hail, sleet and rain. It became necessary to prepare against any attack that might be made upon us. The following disposition was made for the night, the wigwam being of a circular form, and the party formed into two divisions, they were placed intermediately, and a space left on each side of the entrance so that those on guard could have a full command of it; the doorway was closed up with a skin, and orders given for no one to go out. The rustling of the trees and the snow falling from them would have made it easy for an enemy to advance close to us without being heard. I had made an exchange with the Indian for his bow and arrows, and at 11 o'clock laid down to rest; but had not been asleep more than ten minutes when I was aroused by a dreadful scream, and exclamation of "O Lord" uttered by Mathew Hughster. Starting at the instant in his sleep, the Indian gave a horrid yell, and a musket was instantly discharged. I could not at this moment but admire the promptiness of the watch, with their arms presented, and swords drawn. This incident, which had like to prove fatal, was occasioned by John Guieme, a foreigner going out. He had mentioned it to the watch. In coming in again, the skin covering of the doorway made a rustling noise. Thomas Taylor, roused by the shriek, fired direct for the entrance, and had not Hughster providentially fallen against him at the moment, which moved the piece from the intended direction, Guieme must inevitably have lost his life. The rest of the night was spent in making covers of deer skin for the locks of the arms.

SATURDAY 26TH JAN. WIND ENE., BLOWING STRONG, WITH SLEET AND FREEZING WEATHER. As soon as it was light the crew were put in motion, and placing an equal number of blankets, shirts and tin pots in each of the wigwams, I gave the Indian to understand that those articles were for the individuals who resided in them. Some more presents were given to him, also some articles attached to the red staff, all of which he seemed to comprehend. At 7 A.M. we left the place intending to return the Monday following. Seeing that the Indian came on, I signified my wish for him to go back; he however continued with us, sometimes running on a little before in a zigzag direction, keeping his eyes to the ice as having a trace to guide him, and once pointed to the westward and laughed. Being now about two-thirds of a mile from the wigwams, he edged in suddenly, and for an instant halted; then took to speed. We at this observed that he had stopped to look at a body lying on the ice. He was still within half a musket-shot, but as his destruction could answer no end, so it would have been equally vain to attempt pursuit; we soon lost sight of him in the haze. On coming up we recognized with horror the bodies of our two unfortunate companions lying about a hundred yards apart; that of the corporal being first, was pierced by one arrow in the back; three arrows had entered that of Bouthland. They were laid out straight with their feet towards the river, and back upwards; their heads were off, and carried away, and no vestige of garments left. Several broken arrows lying about and a quantity of bread, which must have been emptied out of their knapsacks; very little blood was visible. This melancholy event naturally much affected all the party; but these feelings soon gave way to sensations of revenge. Although I had no doubt as to the possibility of finding out the route they had taken, yet prudence called on me to adopt another line of conduct. As I could have no doubt that our movements had been watched, which the cross track, observed in coming up, evinced, my mind consequently became alarmed for the safety of those left with the sledges, and hence made it of the utmost moment to join them without loss of time. Prior to entering the river the people were refreshed with some rum and bread, and formed into a line of march, those having fire arms being in the front and rear, those with cutlasses remaining in the centre, and all charged to keep as close together as the intricacies would permit. On opening the first point of the river head, one of the men said he observed an Indian look round the second point, and fall back; on coming up, we perceived that two men had certainly been there, and retreated; we afterwards saw them at times at a good distance before us; the tracks showed that they had shoes on; this caused considerable perplexity; the guides (and indeed all the party) were of opinion that the Indians had seen the sledges and that those two were returning down the river to draw us into a trammel; for they supposed a body of them to [be] conveniently posted to take advantage of us in some difficult pass. These conjectures were probable. They strongly urged my taking to the woods as being more safe; although this was certainly true, it would have been attended with great loss of time, for from the depth and softness of the snow, we could not possibly perform it under two days; and as the immediate joining my people was paramount to every other consideration—for our conjectures might be erroneous—and I was in this instance fain to suspect that curiosity had predominated over the obligations of duty, and that want of consideration had led our men up to view the pond, I therefore continued on by the river side. On seeing excrement recently evacuated it was found on examination to contain particles of bread. This relieved the mind, for the Indians do not use this diet. At noon we arrived at the fireplace, and found all well after having spent four hours in unutterable anxiety for their fate. The two men that had acted so imprudently were easily discovered by the sweat that rolled down their faces; being made acquainted with the uneasiness they had occasioned, contrition for their misconduct was manifest. Whilst the party dined on pork, bread and rum, I pondered on the late events, and what in the present juncture was best to be done; my thoughts often wandered to the pond, but after half an hour's reflection, the following considerations fixed me in the resolution of proceeding down the river: 1st, it appeared to me next to a certainty that a numerous body of natives resided in the environs and outlets of the pond; taking this for granted, the hazard would have been greater than prudence would justify, for, after their perpetration, was it not to be supposed they would anticipate our conduct according to their diabolical system? I could not therefore entertain any hope of securing their persons without bloodshed, which would frustrate all future expectation of their reconciliation and civilization, the grand object in view. It will not be considered improper to remark that the very nature of the service intrusted to my care required the test of faith, and the danger increased by the sincere wish of rendering acts of friendship on our part whilst a malignant inveteracy subsists in the hearts and actuates the natives to deeds most horrid. 2nd, the state of the weather promising

31

a rapid thaw, which would render our retreat down the river impracticable; this, with the local situation of this part of the Exploits, were cogent reasons to follow the plan of descending the river. The thawing of the ice and snow, and waters from the interior causing the ice already to founder from the banks so as to render it impossible to conduct the sledges, the knapsacks were filled with as much provisions as they could contain, and, taking with us rum for three days, we commenced our return, obliged to leave everything else behind.

Walking with swollen legs, often knee-deep in icy water, Lieutenant Buchan and his men made the return journey to the mouth of the river in strenuous marches of eighteen to twenty-two miles a day. Exhausted, cold, and wet, they reached the schooner *Adonis* at noon on January 30. It was a great relief to climb aboard and change into dry clothes.

CHAPTER THREE

Shananditti later explained the reasons for Buchan's failure, and for the deaths of the two marines. She also related the grisly aftermath of what happened to the severed heads. (See illustration next page, Shananditti's sketch of the events.) The tragedy could quickly have escalated had not Buchan's strength of character and clarity of judgement prevailed. When his men found the headless and naked bodies of their two companions, they were hot for revenge. It would have been an easy matter to track down the fleeing Beothucks, whose footprints were plainly visible in the snow. Had they done so, there is no doubt about the inevitable outcome: a vicious blood bath in which many women and children would have died.

Buchan acted wisely in diverting the attention of his men to the safety of those left behind with the supplies. As he correctly reasoned, pursuit would have destroyed any future hope of a reconciliation. It could not have been an easy decision for him to make, considering the anger of his men and their demands for revenge.

Throughout this difficult journey Buchan demonstrated his patience, endurance, and cool-headedness. A disciplined leader, he set a good example for the others to follow. He did not bear a grudge against the Beothucks, or even blame them for what happened. As he wrote afterwards, "My opinion of the natives is not the worse for the fatal circumstance that has occurred, for I do not think the deed to have been premeditated. It is nevertheless impossible for me to assign a reason so to be freed from all doubt of the real

They reach this at night and encamp in the woods & right of not running across the Lake

Reach this before day light and then camp for several days with Capt. B. on ice when encamps and found them here and found

L a k e

Indians crossing the Lake

Island

half a days march across

encampment

A small party that were encamped here remov'd join the main body of the tribe

The whole tribe encamp'd here and remain the Winter

Captain Buchan's visit to the Red Indians in 1810-11 when the two marines were killed

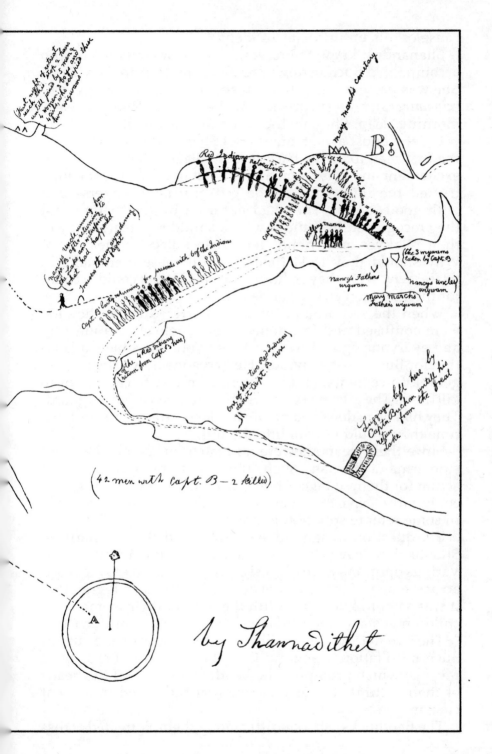

first night retreat...
...made as till... 2 here...
...till... 2 5 men & ...
...9 women & 5 men...
...Indians who destroyed...
...two wigwams

mary march's cemitary

B

Red Indians retreating

...body party on the ice to surprise the Indians...very Mamus

after Kill

Capt. Buchan

Kill'd Mamus

Nancys uncle running for life after receiving Capt to shew him what had happened

Indians throng around wigwam

the 3 wigwams taken by Capt. B

Nancy's Fathers wigwam

Mary March's Father's wigwam

Nancy's uncles wigwam

Capt. B party returning of presents with 6 of the Indians

the 4 Red Indians return from Capt. B here

one of the two Red Indians desert Capt. B here

Luggage left here by Capta Buchan untill his return from the great Lake

(42 men with Capt. B – 2 killed)

A

by Shannadithet

cause of this unfortunate accident."

Shananditti knew the reason, since it was her uncle who accompanied Buchan down the river and back to the village. She was present when Buchan surrounded the "wigwams" (*mamateeks*) and surprised the Beothucks from an early morning sleep. She saw the two marines killed.

Chief Nonosbawsut, another of Shananditti's uncles, was the first man to arrive back in the village. There was much excitement and confusion about what to do. Everyone mistrusted the intentions of the gift-bearing strangers—and with good reason. They had not seen Buchan before, but they recognized his guides with a shudder of fear. Many of their relatives and friends had been killed by these men. Why should they trust them now? If these men came in peace, why were they so heavily armed? What could account for their sudden change of heart?

When the second and third man arrived back, they too were confused and frightened. The chief called a meeting and everyone agreed there was only one possible explanation for Buchan's behaviour. He had gone down the river to get reinforcements, and he intended either to capture or to kill them. The gifts were a clever plan to catch them off guard. They had been deceived before by clever stratagems, but this time they would not fall into the trap.

Since their weapons were no match for the muskets and side arms of Buchan's men, there was only one course of action for them to take. They must pack up everything they could carry, leave the village as quickly as possible, and hide in some remote spot of the forest.

The question arose about what to do with the two marines. Should they leave them behind, or take them with them? Various opinions were expressed and it was not easy to reach an agreement. Finally it was decided, with deep regret, that it was safer to kill them. With the lives of their women and children at stake, they could not have decided otherwise.

The two marines were killed and their heads were cut off. Such mutilation seems ruthless, but it was not cruelty or revenge which prompted the Beothucks to cut off the heads of their victims. It was a ceremonial act rooted in ancient custom.

The Beothucks, Shananditti among them, retreated across

the frozen lake to the north shore with all possible haste. But with the snow and the children they could not travel quickly. Their aim was to warn the other scatterd families along the lake and to ask them to join them in some distant spot of concealment for the remaining six weeks of winter. This would also increase their numbers—an important consideration, since they believed that Buchan might press an attack.

About nine miles along the lake they reached the site of two more *mamateeks*. Here they were joined by five men, four women, three boys and four girls. Although it was midnight, they rested for only two hours before continuing.

They travelled all night along the north shore of the lake and reached a point opposite a small island just before daylight. Here they rested for a day and a half, hoping that Shananditti's uncle would catch up with them. They had no way of knowing how long he would remain with Buchan, or if in fact he was still alive.

In the illustration Shananditti's uncle is running across the lake. The small arch behind him represents the pants which Buchan gave him as a present. He discarded them because he could run faster without them.

When her uncle rejoined them, he told his strange story. His report of another body of armed men at the supply depot only confirmed their suspicions that Buchan had gone for reinforcements. There could be no doubt that he had been planning a surprise attack.

Since an attack was still possible, they continued west along the shore; by evening they had reached the half-way point on the lake. They camped there for the night, and early the next morning headed south across the lake to the opposite shore. A note on Shananditti's drawing informs us that it was "half a days march."

When they reached the shore, they retreated some distance into the woods and set up five *mamateeks*. Later another family who were camped farther down the lake came to join them. As the drawing indicates, all of the Beothucks spent the rest of the winter at this site.

Behind the five *mamateeks* of the winter encampment is a small curious circle labelled "A." There is a line in the circle and a large dot at the top of the line. A similar small circle and line occurs at "B" on the north east shore. A dotted line connects the small circle A with the large circle A. It is clear that the second circle A is an enlargement of the other two smaller circles.

The details of the large circle are easy to recognize. The line in the centre of the circle is a pole, and the object on the top of the pole is a human head. There are two lines on the rim of the circle and this represents a ceremonial path. Notes written on Shananditti's drawing tell us what happened:

"Marines head stuck on a pole, around which the Indians danced and sang two hours in the woods at A, they having carried the head with them: the other marines head they left at B, and on their return there in the spring, they danced and sang round it in like manner."

Asked for an exact census of the people in the winter camp, Shananditti gave these figures:

In the first settlement, that which Lt. Buchan visited, there were in one *mamateek* 4 men, 5 women and 6 children 15
In another *mamateek* 4 men, 2 women, 3 girls and 3 other children 12
In another *mamateek* 3 men, 3 women, 2 single women and 7 children .... <u>15</u>
                                                                                42

In the two *mamateeks* of the second settlement, that on the north shore of the lake, were 3 women, 4 men and 6 children 13
In the third settlement, that at the southwest end of the lake, one *mamateek* housed 2 men, 4 women and 3 children 9
Another housed 3 men, 3 women and 2 children .... <u>8</u>
                                                                    Total 72

There is a discrepancy between these figures and those on Shananditti's drawing. In the second settlement, the figures on the drawing indicate sixteen persons, not thirteen.

Whether the total population was seventy-two or seventy-five, the figure is tragic testimony to the fate of the Beothucks. Once a strong nation of many thousands occupying the whole of Newfoundland, they were now reduced to a frightened handful hiding in a remote corner of the forest. In 1811 when Shananditti was ten years old, the Beothucks were only a few footsteps from extinction. If they had trusted Buchan, would their fate have been any different?

When spring came, all their food was gone and there was not enough game in the area to feed the seventy-two persons. Reluctantly they returned to the first village, where they had hidden a stock of venison. Then some of the men paddled down the river to a storehouse where they had left more venison. As they approached the place, their mistrust and fear of Buchan and his men was still strong. What they did was recorded by Buchan, who later visited the site: "I was surprised to find that the skin coverings in that part of the store fronting the river and the inland side, were perforated with many arrows; this circumstance led me to conclude that they had come down in their canoes, and that some of them had taken a station on the bank, and had shot their arrows at the store, to ascertain whether we might not be concealed in it." In the year following Buchan's expedition, twenty-two Beothucks died of starvation.

Eight years would pass before the Beothucks would see David Buchan again. They would see him only from a distance and under very odd and painful circumstances. In the intervening years he would be promoted from lieutenant to commander and he would receive many citations for his courage and conduct during the fire which destroyed most of St. John's in 1816 and for his leadership during the famine and lawlessness which followed the fire. A report said of him: "He was then in command of H.M.S. *Pike*, and during the winter he put all his crew on short allowance to relieve the distress of the inhabitants. For his humane and praiseworthy conduct during this trying season, he was presented with a most flattering address of thanks by the Grand Jury, and also with a service of plate by the inhabitants."

When David Buchan returned from his journey in 1811, he remarked that he had seen a light-haired woman living among the Beothucks. "Conceive my astonishment at beholding a female bearing all the appearance of a European, with light sandy hair, and features strongly similar to the French, apparently about 22 years of age, with an infant which she carried in her cossack, her demeanour differing materially from the others. Instead of that sudden change from surprise and dismay to acts of familiarity, she never uttered a word, nor did she recover from the terror our sudden and unexpected visit had thrown them into."

Shananditti was later quizzed about this unusual woman: had the Beothucks ever kidnapped a white child? Surprisingly, Shananditti denied any knowledge of this woman. Her answer may have been a lie prompted by fear of punishment, or she may simply not have remembered the woman. Shananditti was only ten at the time of Buchan's visit and the woman may have died shortly after.

The identity of the woman with the light hair has never been discovered. Was she kidnapped, or is there another explanation?

In 1576 five sailors had deserted from the ship of Sir Martin Frobisher. They had stolen a boat, rowed ashore, and joined the Beothucks. Nothing more was seen of them, but thirty-six years later John Guy, the first governor of the new colony, saw their sandy-haired sons. The woman whom Buchan saw may have been a descendant of these sailors. Or, since the Europeans "kidnapped" so many Beothucks, the favour may have been returned. There was only one other instance of this in the entire three hundred years of settlement. The details of the story were written down by James Howley, who heard it in 1886 from a very old fisherman, and it is a tale of love and suffering.

"Once a crew of fishermen were somewhere up the Bay [Bay of Exploits], making what is termed a 'winter's work,' i.e. cutting timber and sawing plank for boat and schooner building, etc. While at work in their saw-pit, beneath a sloping bank and close to the woods, they were annoyed by someone throwing snow balls at them, from the top of the bank. Thinking it was some friends from another camp who were amusing themselves in this way, they did not pay much heed at first, but after a while, as the annoyance continued, one of the party determined to investigate. He climbed up the bank and entered the woods, and not returning again, his companions, after a long delay, believing something must have happened to him, went in search; he was nowhere to be found. They soon came across footprints in the snow, apparently made by Indians, and then unmistakable signs of a struggle. It was very evident to them that their unfortunate companion had been seized by the Red men and forcibly carried off. In vain they searched all around, but the Indians had a good start of them and had gone away into the interior with their captive. Nothing more was heard of the missing man till a year or more had elapsed. One day some fishermen, including some of the same party, were rowing along shore in the vicinity, when they were suddenly surprised by seeing a man rush out of the woods, jump into the water and make towards them, at the same time making signals and calling some of them by name.

"Although dressed in deerskin and besmeared with red ochre, like all the Indians, they nevertheless recognized their long lost friend, and rowed towards him. In the meantime, just as he gained the boat a number of Indians appeared on the beach, wildly gesticulating and discharged a flight of arrows at the party. One, a woman, holding aloft an infant, waded out to her waist in the water, and entreating the fugitive by voice and gesture to come back, but seeing it was of no avail, and that the boat into which he had clambered, was moving away from the shore she drew from her girdle a large knife, and deliberately cut the infant in two parts, one of which she flung with all her might towards the retreating boat, the other, she pressed to her bosom, in an agony of grief.

"The fisherman now told his story, which was to the effect that upon climbing over the bank, and entering the woods he was suddenly pounced upon bound and gagged before he could make any outcry, by the Indians who were concealed in a hollow close by. They then made a precipitate retreat, carrying him with them, away into the interior. For a long while they kept a close watch upon him never leaving him for a moment unguarded. One of the Indian women who took a particular fancy to him, presumably because he was a red-headed man, was given him to wife in Indian fashion, and in course of time a child was born to them. The tribe wandered about the interior from place to place, and believing now that their captive had become thoroughly reconciled to his surroundings, they relaxed their vigilance. On again approaching the seacoast and seeing some of his old friends and associates, his natural desire to regain his liberty and return to his fellow whites, overcame all other considerations. He made a dash for the boat and as we have seen was fortunate enough to escape the arrows and rejoin his friends."

CHAPTER FOUR

When Shananditti was fifteen, she witnessed the murder of a
Beothuck woman by John Peyton, Sr. On a sketch which
records this brutal crime (see page 44) there are two important notes. They identify the killer by name, and they show
that murders continued until a very late date. The first note
reads: "Accompanied with 2 others, old Mr. Peyton killed a
woman at A 14 or 15 years ago on the Exploits River." The
second note reads: "Showing that the murder of them was
going on in 1816."

In Shananditti's sketch, the line on the river indicates that
Mr. Peyton and two others came up the river to the campsite.
The three lines radiating from A show the escape routes of
the fleeing Beothucks. Some crossed the river to an island,
some ran up the river on the ice, and some circled through
the woods and rejoined the others up the river on the opposite bank. It would appear that a brief warning of Peyton's
approach was given; otherwise, more would have died. The
woman who was killed may have been ill or too weak from
starvation to run.

It was a vicious crime, and John Peyton, Sr., as the father of
Magistrate John Peyton, Jr., must certainly have been well
acquainted with the government's policy to save the Beothucks from extinction.

Two years after this killing, Shananditti was the helpless
witness to yet another tragedy, a double tragedy this time:
the capture of her aunt Demasduit and the murder of Chief
Nonosbawsut, who was Demasduit's husband and Shananditti's dearest uncle. And again the Peytons were the cause.

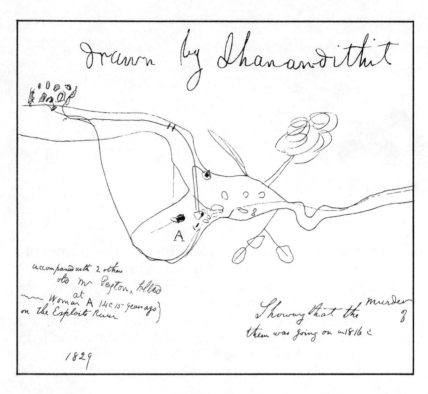

drawn by Shanandithit

accompanied with 2 others
who mr Peyton killed
at
Woman A 14 c 15 years ago)
on the Exploits River

Showing that the murder of
them was going on in 1816 &

1829

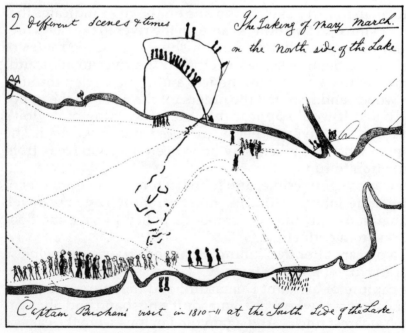

2 different Scenes & times   The Taking of mary march.
                                    on the North side of the Lake

Captain Buchan's visit in 1810–11 at the South Side of the Lake.

44

Chief Nonosbawsut stood over six and a half feet tall, and was known for his wisdom as well as for his exceptional strength. He believed that he could only save his people from their slow but certain death by bringing all the scattered families together to protect each other and help each other hunt and gather food. Had he not been killed, his plan might have worked.

Shananditti's sketch (below left) is a condensed version of two tragic scenes. The right half repeats in larger scale part of pages 34-35. It shows Buchan and his men, accompanied by four Beothucks, marching in single file towards the outflowing river. Two marines remain behind, and four Beothucks are approaching them. It was these four who later killed the marines. There are two Beothucks standing on the shore a short distance away, but it is not clear whether they are standing up or lying down. The three *mamateeks* are shown this time with many short strokes beside them. These represent the number of people left in the village at the time.

The left half of the sketch refers to the capture of Demasduit and the murder of her husband, Nonosbawsut, the last Beothuck chief. The sketch shows his dead body lying on the ice. The consequences of this scene meant even more suffering and sorrow, since the capture of the mother ended not only in her own death but also in the death of her baby who was left behind. The death of the chief meant the certain end for all the rest.

Demasduit was captured on March 5, 1819 by Judge John Peyton, Jr. and his father John Peyton, Sr. at Red Indian Lake. (Her Beothuck name was pronounced "De-mas-do-weet"; she was renamed Mary March after the month of her capture.)

How this all came about is a strange, tangled story. Many of the details were hotly disputed afterward, and in testifying before a Grand Jury the men in Peyton's party who witnessed the death of the chief did not agree on several important details. There are at least four different published versions about what happened, two of them by John Peyton, Jr.

An entry in the diary of John Peyton, Jr., relates how the tragedy began:

On the night of the 18th of September, 1818, between the hours of 12 and half-past 1, the wild Indians cut adrift from the wharf at Lower Sandy Point, Exploits, a boat loaded with salmon. The boat was found the next day, stranded on an island near Grego, or gray gull Island,—sails gone and considerable other property stolen or destroyed. Guns, pistols, watch, money and many articles of personal apparel too numerous to mention. Cargo but little damaged.

Shananditti had been present at the time the boat was stolen, and she later recounted all the details of the occurrence. She and a number of others watched Peyton's movements for several days from atop a high wooded hill behind his house. It was called Canoe Hill because it looked like a canoe turned upside down. Shananditti pointed out a tall birch tree on the summit which was used as a lookout. She told Peyton that several men were hidden in their canoe under the wharf when he made his last inspection of the boat. They watched him walk on the boards over their heads. Since it was dark, it was easy for them to tow the boat away unseen.

The following events were written down by James Howley, who heard it, as he states, "from the lips of the late John Peyton, J.P. of Twillingate, himself the actual captor of the Beothuck woman."

The circumstance which lead to the capture of Mary March is related thus by Mr Peyton. While prosecuting the salmon fishery and fur trade in the bay and river of Exploits, he was much tormented by the depredations of the Indians, who came, usually in the night time, and pilfered everything they could lay hands upon. The articles stolen were not often of great value, and consisted generally of such things as knives, axes, traps, hooks, lines, rope, canvass etc. Annoying as this undoubtedly was Mr Peyton bore with it for a long time, and without using any retaliative measures. At length the Indians became so emboldened as to commit a theft and act of destruction of more than ordinary character, which he could not overlook. Mr P. was living at the time at Lower Sandy Point, in the Bay of Exploits, his house and stores stood upon the sloping bank of the river and a long wharf, built on piers, extended from the shore out to the deep water. On this occasion, his large open boat, loaded with the season's produce, lay at the head of the wharf, ready to proceed down the Bay to

46

market. It was one of those old style of boats, open amidship, with a cuddy at the forward and after ends, somewhat on the lines of the ancient caraval. Besides the cargo of salmon and furs, Mr P. had stowed away in the cuddies his clothes, bedding, and several articles of value, including two silver watches, and some coins which were in his vest pockets, and there were also two guns and ammunition, culinary and other utensils aboard for use on the voyage.

Everything being in readiness, he and his crew were awaiting daylight and the turn of the tide to proceed on their journey. The night was very dark, and knowing that the Indians were about, a strict watch was kept, but seeing no prospect of a favourable time up till past midnight, he directed his men to lie down and take a rest while he himself would remain on guard. He took frequent turns up and down the wharf, and at one time said he thought he descried a dark object lying on the beach not far off which he was about to investigate, when one of his men assured him it was a splitting table that had been left there during the day, so he did not pay further heed to it. As the night drew on and everything appeared quiet, he concluded nothing would be disturbed during the few remaining hours before dawn, so feeling somewhat tired himself, he took one more thorough survey and then retired to the house to rest awhile. He threw himself down on a couch without removing his clothing, but he was so restless and uneasy he could not sleep. An hour or so may have elapsed, when he jumped up and again visited the wharf. To his great mortifiction he found the boat with all its effects gone, and in the inky darkness could find no clue to the direction taken by the marauders.

He now called all his crew, and as soon as daylight made its appearance, started in pursuit. After many hours search they at length found the boat hauled up in a small creek at the mouth of Charles' Brook, away down on the other side of the bay. She was completely rifled, everything of a portable nature, including the cordage and sails being carried off. The guns alone, battered and broken, and otherwise rendered perfectly useless, were found in the bed of the brook not far away. To follow up the trail just then would be very difficult and most probably futile. Mr Peyton accordingly proceeded to St. John's and laid the whole matter before the authorities whom, he said, were very reluctant to believe the story. The Governor, Sir Charles Hamilton, however, gave full credence to it, and empowered Mr Peyton to search for his stolen property, and if possible try and capture one of the Indians alive.

Armed with this authority he chose the following winter, 1819, to make the attempt. At that season of the year the travelling on the frozen surface of the river would be easiest, and the Indians who would have retired to their winter quarters in the interior would be least suspicious of being disturbed. He chose the month of March to make the journey, this month being always considered the best for winter travelling, owing to the settled character of the snow and hardness of the surface. With half a dozen of his hardy furriers he set out to traverse the Exploits River, but instead of following its entire course to Red Indian Lake, as Buchan had done, he turned off to the right some distance below, rightly conjecturing that by so doing he would strike the lake near the head of the N.E. Arm, where he expected the Indians would be encamped. His party reached the shore of the lake one afternoon late, but in time to observe the smoke of three wigwams on the north side, nearly opposite to where Buchan had found them encamped. Although the night proved intensely cold Peyton would not allow his men to kindle a fire lest the Indians should detect their presence. They sheltered themselves as best they could in a deep gully near the mouth of a small brook, and at the first appearance of daylight were on the move towards the wigwams, where they arrived before the occupants had yet awakened. They then surrounded them, but the Indians aroused, darted forth and fled in all directions, before any of them could be secured. Being, as he said, a young active man at that time, Peyton determined to try and outrun some of them. Divesting himself of superfluous clothing, he gave chase to the nearest one on the lake, who seemed to lag somewhat behind the rest, and soon found that he gained considerably on this individual. After a while the Indian began to show evident signs of exhaustion, and finally stopped and made supplication for mercy. She, for it proved to be a woman, tore open her deer-skin cossack exposing her bosoms in an appeal to his manhood. In order to reassure her and allay her fears, he cast his gun aside into a bank of soft snow and then leisurely approached her with signs of amity, he laid hold of her and endeavoured to lead her back. He was now considerably in advance of his party who were following on behind, and as he tried to drag the woman with him some of the Indians turned and approached him. One powerful looking fellow came up furiously brandishing a bright new axe with which he would certainly have killed Mr Peyton had not his men just then arrived on the scene and prevented it. The Indians then moved off and the party, taking the woman along with them returned to the wigwams which with their contents they thoroughly overhauled. One of the wigwams was covered with the stolen boat sails, the other two as usual with birch bark. Inside were found many of the pilfered articles belonging to Mr Peyton, besides several others similarly appropriated from other parties. They consisted of kettles, knives, axes, fish hooks and fishing lines etc. Some of the axes were quite new, and Mr Peyton afterwards learned that they had been stolen from a store in White Bay the previous fall.

The watches had been broken into small pieces, which together with the coins were strung on deer-skin thongs, passed through holes drilled in them, and presumably intended for necklaces, amulets or some such adornment.

Mr Peyton did not think there were more than fourteen or fifteen individuals in these three wigwams, but it was impossible to count them as they darted through the woods.

His party now retreated as they had come taking the woman with them, keeping a close watch all the time lest she should escape which she made attempts to do. Once while all were asleep she nearly succeeded. Taking off her outer deer-skin robe and placing it on the snow she noiselessly crawled along, dragging the skin after her to deaden the sound of her footsteps, or obliterate her track in the snow. She had gained a considerable distance when her absence was noticed, but she was soon recaptured and brought back. After this she made no further attempt but kept close to Mr P. all the time, as though for protection, no doubt recognizing in him the leader of the party and a man superior in every way to his fellows.

This is John Peyton, Jr.'s version of what happened. It seems straightforward, but he neglects to mention that Mary March was holding a baby when he chased her, and he makes no mention of the shooting of her husband. James Howley, who recorded Peyton's story, was a trained historian and a meticulous scholar, and it seems certain that he transcribed Peyton's words with a high degree of reliability.

There is only one conclusion we can draw from Peyton's account. He was suppressing the truth. Why did he find this necessary? Did he feel guilty or ashamed of what he had done? Was he afraid of implicating himself in a criminal offence?

There is another aspect of Peyton's story which makes it difficult to believe what he says. His reasons for doing what he did are not plausible. He says that he went into the interior to recover his stolen goods, but the expense of outfitting a party of men to make the long arduous journey far exceeded the cost of the items he hoped to recover. He says that he showed amity towards Mary March (Demasduit), but he dragged her off, separated her from her child and killed her husband. This was hardly the way to win her friendship, or to demonstrate the good will advised by the governor. It seems more likely that he was thinking of the £100 sterling reward for the capture of a living Beothuck. This would more than cover the cost of his stolen articles.

Finally, there is Peyton's portrait of the Beothucks as habitual thieves. He does not mention that the settlers repeatedly stole furs and salmon from the Beothucks. The River and Bay of Exploits were the traditional fishing grounds of the Beothucks. Peyton and the other settlers were intruders; they had no legal rights to the land or the fish.

CHAPTER FIVE

Although John Peyton, Jr. wanted to hide the truth, some of his men did not remain tight-lipped. Word soon spread that someone had killed the Beothuck chief when Mary March was captured. Whether someone laid a formal charge against Peyton, or whether he requested an investigation to clear his name, is not known.

The death of Chief Nonosbawsut was taken as a serious matter. Thanks to the indefatigable letter writing of Magistrate John Bland over a number of years, the murder of a Beothuck had finally become an indictable offence. If John Peyton, Sr. were convicted of the murder, he would receive a stiff sentence. The fact that a Grand Jury was called to pass judgement shows the seriousness with which the legal profession regarded the matter.

Unfortunately there is no record or description of what the Peytons did or said at the trial, but we do have the statement which Newman W. Hoyles, the foreman of the Grand Jury, read in the Court House on May 25, 1819. A great deal can be inferred from this statement:

The Grand Jury beg leave to state to the Court that they have, as far as it was possible, investigated the unfortunate circumstances which occasioned the loss of life to one of the Red Indian Tribe near the River of Exploits in the late rencontre which took place between the deceased and John Peyton, Sr., in the presence of Peyton, Jr., his son, and a party of their own men, to the number of ten in all, and in sight of several Indians of the same tribe. The Grand Jury are of opinion that no malice preceded the transaction, and that there was no intention on the part of Peyton's party to get possession of any of them by such violence as would occasion bloodshed. But it appears that the deceased came by his death in consequence of the attack on Peyton, Sr., and his subsequent obstinacy, and not desisting when repeatedly menaced by some of the party for that purpose, and the peculiar situation of the Peytons and their men, was such as to warrant their acting on the defensive. At the same time that the Grand Jury declare these opinions arising from the only evidence brought before them, they cannot but regret the want of other evidence to corroborate the foregoing, viewing it as they do a matter of the first importance, and which calls for the most complete establishment of innocence on the part of the Peyton's and their men, they therefore recommend that four of the party should be brought round at the end of the fishing season for that purpose.

It is clear from this statement that the only evidence presented to the Grand Jury was the testimony of John Peyton, Jr. and his father, who could hardly be expected to give evidence damaging to themselves. Under these circumstances, it is difficult to see how the Grand Jury could have reached any kind of decision.

John Peyton, Jr. must be seen for what he was—rash, wilful, and greedy. He wanted the reward money for the capture of a live Beothuck. (Those who offered the reward did not stipulate male or female, sick or well.) The money "justified" the use of force and murder; all Peyton's actions point to this one inescapable conclusion.

The jury was gullible and biased. They had a distorted view of their function in the judicial process. They were concerned, not with the injustice and harm done to the Beothucks, but with "the most complete establishment of innocence on the part of the Peyton's and their men." So much for truth and justice.

Two days after the Grand Jury handed down their verdict, John Peyton, Jr. wrote a long letter to the governor, Sir Charles Hamilton. Why he did this is not at all clear. A close look at the letter suggests several possible motives.

The first part of the letter contains a list of the various items stolen during the five years previous to the capture of Mary March. These include traps, nets, sails, fishing tackle, etc. The cost of each item is carefully recorded, and there is a statement of the inconvenience suffered for each loss. Peyton still seemed concerned about proving his innocence, although the repeated thefts by the Beothucks could not have justified his actions.

The second part of the letter contains a vivid description of the chief's struggles to save his wife, including the multiple wounds he suffered before his death. Peyton states that the chief was shot by three different persons and he does not indicate which persons actually killed him, leaving it impossible to place the blame on any one person. But more important, is this a true account of what really happened, or is it a crafty fabrication?

The third part of the letter is an appeal to the governor for a very large sum of money to pay Peyton's expenses for a return trip to the interior. He assures the governor that he can make friends with the Beothucks and win their trust.

Here is part of this letter; see how carefully Peyton defends himself, and how he appeals to the governor's charity and humanity:

On the first of March 1819, I left my house accompanied by my father and eight of my own men with a most anxious desire of being able to take some of the Indians and thus through them open a friendly communication with the rest, everyone was ordered by me not upon any account to commence hostilities without my positive orders. On the 2nd March we came up with a few wigwams frequented by the Indians during the spring and autumn for the purpose of killing deer. On the 3rd we saw a fireplace by the side of the brook where some Indians had slept a few days before. On the 4th, at 10 o'clock we came to a storehouse belonging to the Indians. On entering it I found five of my cat traps, set, as I supposed, to protect their venison from the cats, and part of my boat's jib, from the fireplace and tracks on the snow we were convinced the Indians had left it the day before in the direction SW. We therefore followed their footing with all possible speed and caution—at 11 o'clock we left the greatest part of our provisions in order to make the more speed, as we were expecting to come up with them very soon—at 1 o'clock we saw where they had slept the night before; we continued to travel till dark. On the 5th we commenced walking as soon as it was day. At eight we came to a large brook which ran about SW. We followed the course of the water which brought us into a very large pond. The wind blowing strong occasioned a heavy drift which destroyed all signs of the tracks; after travelling about one and a half miles I discovered the footing of two or more Indians quite fresh; we imagined they were gone into the woods for the purpose of partridge shooting. I ordered the men to keep close together and keep a good lookout towards the woods. On proceeding a little further I saw a high point projecting on the pond, and on looking over it very carefully I discovered one Indian coming towards us, and three more going the contrary way at some considerable distance. I fell back and told our party what I had seen; their curiosity being excited I could not restrain them from endeavouring to get sight of the Indians. I was not then certain there were no more in the same course I saw the one in. I could not tell at this time whether the Indian I saw was a male or female. I showed myself on the point openly. When the Indian discovered me she for a moment was motionless. She screamed out as soon as she appeared to make me out, and ran off. I immediately pursued her, but did not gain on her until I had taken off my rackets and jacket. When I came up with her fast, she kept looking back at me over her shoulder I then dropped my gun on the snow and held up my hands to show her I had no gun, and on my pointing to my gun which was then some distance behind me, she stopped. I did the same and endeavoured to convince her I would not hurt her. I then advanced and gave her my hand, she gave hers to me and to all my party as they came up. We then saw seven or eight Indians repeatedly running off and on the pond, as I imagined from their wigwams. Shortly after three Indians came running towards us—when they came within about 200 or 300 yds. from us they made a halt. I advanced towards them with the woman, and on her calling to the Indians two of their party came down to us, the third halted again about 100 yards distant. I ordered one of the men to examine one of the Indians that did come to us, having observed something under his cassock, which proved to be a hatchet, which the man took from him,—the two Indians came and took hold of me by the arms endeavouring to force me away. I cleared myself as well as I could still having the woman in my hand. The Indian from whom the hatchet was taken attempted to lay hold of three different guns, but without effect. He at last succeeded in getting hold of my father's gun, and tried to force it from him, and in the attempt to get his gun he and my father got off nearly fifty yards from me in the direction of the woods; at the same time the other Indian who attacked my father grasped him by the throat. My father drew a bayonet with the hope of intimidating the Indian. It had not the desired effect, for he only made a savage grin at it. I then called for one of the men to strike him, which he did across the hands with his gun; he still held on my father till he was struck on the head, when he let my father go, and either struck at or made a grasp at the man who struck him, which he evaded by falling under the hand. At the same time this encounter was taking place, the third Indian who had halted about 100 yards kept at no great distance from us, and there were seven or eight more repeatedly running out from the woods on the look out, and no greater distance from us than 300 yards. The Indian turned again on my father and made a grasp at his throat—my father extricated himself and on his retreat the Indian still forcing on him, fired. I ordered one of the men to defend my father, when two guns were fired, but the guns were all fired so close together that I did not know till some time after that more than one had been fired. The rest of the Indians fled immediately on the fall of the unfortunate one. Could we have intimidated or persuaded him to leave us, or even have seen the others go off, we should have been most happy to have spared using violence, but when it was remembered that our small party were in the heart of the Indians' country, one hundred miles from any European settlement, and that there were in our sight at times as many Indians as our party amounted to, and we could not ascertain how many were in the woods that we did not see, it could not be avoided with safety to ourselves. Had destruction been our object we might have carried it much further. Nor should I have brought this woman to the capital to Your Excellency, nor should I offer my services for the ensuing summer, had I wantonly put an end to the unfortunate man's existence, as in the case of success in taking any more during the summer and opening a friendly intercourse with them, I must be discovered.

My object was and still is to endeavour to be on good terms with the Indians for the protection of my property, and the rescuing of that tribe of our fellow creatures from the misery and persecution they are exposed to in the interior from the Micmacs, and on the exterior by the Whites. With this impression on my mind I offer my services to the Government for the ensuing summer and implore Your Excellency to lend me any assistance you may think proper. I cannot afford to do much at my own expense, having nothing but what I work for, the expenses of doing anything during the summer would be less than the winter, as it will not be safe ever to attempt going into their country with so small a crew as I had with me last winter. Still these expenses are much greater than I can afford, as nothing effectual can be expected to be done under £400. Unless Your Excellency should prefer sending an expedition on the service out of the fleet, in which case I would leave the woman at Your Excellency's disposal, but should I be appointed to cruise the summer for them, and which I could not do and find men and necessaries under £400, I have not the least doubt but that I shall, through the medium of the woman I now have, be enabled to open an intercourse with them, nor is it all improbable but that she will return with us again if she can to procure an infant child she left behind her. I beg to assure Your Excellency from my acquaintance with the bays and the place of resort for the Indians during the summer, that I am most confident of succeeding in the plan here laid down.

After what Peyton did, it is not possible that he really believed he could act as a goodwill ambassador. At the very sight of him, the Beothucks would flee in terror. In their eyes he was a kidnapper and accomplice to a murderer. There was no way he could gain their trust and friendship.

Peyton's reasons for going back into the interior are unconvincing, if not completely fallacious. He says that he wanted to be on good terms with the Beothucks to protect his property. There were much easier ways to do this. He says that he wanted to rescue the Beothucks from the misery and persecution of the Micmacs and people like himself, but he had no control over the Micmacs and very little control over his own men. If other fishermen and trappers from the coast wanted to travel into the interior, he could not stop them, and he could not remove the prejudice and malice from their minds.

The governor did not hand over £400 to finance Peyton's dubious scheme.

CHAPTER SIX

The truth about what happened on the frozen surface of Red Indian Lake did not emerge until ten years after the capture of Mary March. It appeared as a letter to the editor in the *Liverpool Mercury* and it was written by one of the men who had accompanied the Peytons on that ill-fated journey into the interior in the winter of 1818.

Mr. E. Slade wrote that he arrived at John Peyton, Jr.'s house on the evening before he left for the interior. He asked Peyton if he could go along and was immediately welcomed as one of the party. He was supplied with a musket, a bayonet, and a pair of snowshoes, as were all the rest.

There were many hardships on the journey. The snow was eight feet deep and the temperature was nineteen degrees below freezing. But the men were in good cheer. They shot deer, partridges, rabbits; they ate well and drank hot rum toddies. In the evenings they built a bivouac of small fir and birch trees and sang songs.

On the evening before their encounter with the Beothucks, Mr. Peyton cautioned the men against "undue violence" and asked them "not to fire on any account." What happened the next day shows that this advice was not taken seriously. (In the following quotation the italics are mine.)

"About three O'clock in the afternoon two men who then led the party were about two hundred yards before the rest; three deer closely followed by a pack of wolves issued from the woods on the left, and bounded across the lake, passing very near the men, whom they totally disregarded. The men incautiously fired at them. We were then about half a mile from the point of land that almost intersected the lake, and in a few minutes we saw it covered with Indians, who instantly retired. The alarm was given; we soon reached the point; about five hundred yards on the other side we saw the Indians' houses, and the Indians, men, women, and children rushing from them, across the lake, here about a mile broad. Hurrying on we quickly came to the houses; when within a short distance from the last house, three men and a woman carrying a child issued forth. One of the men took the infant from her, and their speed soon convinced us of the futility of pursuit; the woman however did not run so fast. Mr ----- loosened his provision bag from his back and let it fall, threw away his gun and hatchet and set off at a speed that soon overtook the woman. One man and myself did the same, except our guns. The rest, picking up our things followed. On overtaking the woman, she instantly fell on her knees, and tearing open the cossack, (a dress composed of deer-skin bound with fur), showing her breasts to prove she was a woman, and begged for mercy. In a few moments we were by Mr -----'s side. Several of the Indians, with the three who had quitted the house with the woman, now advanced, while we retreated towards the shore. At length we stopped and they did the same. After a pause three of them laid down their bows with which they were armed, and came within two hundred yards. We then presented our guns, intimating that not more than one would be allowed to approach. They retired and fetched their arms, when one, the ill-fated husband of Mary March, our captive, *advanced with a branch of fir tree (spruce) in his hand.* When about ten yards off he stopped and made a long oration. He spoke at least ten minutes; towards the last his gestures became very animated and his eye 'shot fire.' He concluded very mildly, and advancing, shook hands with many of the party—then he attempted to take his wife from us; being opposed in this he drew from beneath his cossack, an axe, the whole of which was finely polished, and brandished it over our heads. On two or three pieces (muskets) being presented, he gave it up to Mr ----- who then intimated that the woman must go with us, but that he might go also if he pleased, and that in the morning both should have their liberty. At the same time two of the

58

men began to conduct her towards the houses. On this being done he became infuriated, and rushing on towards her strove to drag her from them; one of the men rushed forward and stabbed him in the back with a bayonet; turning round, at a blow he laid the fellow at his feet; the next instant he knocked down another and rushing on—like a child laid him on his back, and seizing his dirk from his belt brandished it over his head; the next instant it would have been buried in him had I not with both hands seized his arm; he shook me off in an instant, while I measured my length on the ice; Mr ----- then drew a pistol from his girdle and fired. The poor wretch first staggered then fell on his face: while writhing in agonies, he seemed for a moment to stop; his muscles stiffened: slowly and gradually he raised himself from the ice, turned round, and with a wild gaze surveyed us all in a circle around him. Never shall I forget the figure he exhibited; his hair hanging on each side of his sallow face; his bushy beard clotted with the blood that flowed from his mouth and nose; his eyes flashing fire, yet with the glass of death upon them,—they fixed on the individual who first stabbed him. Slowly he raised the hand that still grasped young -----'s dagger, till he raised it considerably above his head, when uttering a yell that made the woods echo, he rushed at him. The man fired as he advanced, and the noble Indian again fell on his face; a few moments struggle, and he lay a stiffened corpse on the icy surface of the limpid waters. The woman for a moment seemed scarcely to notice the corpse, in a few minutes however, she showed a little motion; but it was not until obliged to leave the remains of her husband that she gave way to grief, and vented her sorrow in the most heartbreaking lamentations. While the scene which I have just described was acting, and which occurred in almost less space than the description can be read, a number of Indians had advanced within a short distance, but seeing the untimely fate of their chief haulted. Mr ----- fired over their heads, and they immediately fled. The banks of the lake, on the other side, were at this time covered with men, women and children, at least several hundreds; but immediately being joined by their companions all disappeared in the woods. We then had time to think. For my part I could scarcely credit my senses, as I beheld the remains of the noble fellow stretched on the ice, crimsoned with his already frozen blood. One of the men then went to the shore for some fir tree boughs to cover the body, which measured as it lay, 6 feet 7½ inches. The fellow who first stabbled him wanted to strip off his cossack (a garment made of deer skin, lined with beaver and other skins, reaching to the knees), but met with so stern a rebuke from ----, that he instantly desisted, and slunk abashed away.

Both ----- and myself bitterly reproached the man who first stabbed the unfortunate native; for though he acted violently, still there was no necessity for the brutal act,—besides the untaught Indian was only doing that which every man ought to do,—he came to rescue his wife from the hands of her captors, and nobly lost his life in his attempt to save her. ----- here declared that he would rather have defeated the object of his journey a hundred times than have sacrificed the life of one Indian. The fellow merely replied, 'it was only an Indian, and he wished he had shot a hundred instead of one.' ".

This account is probably more accurate than the previous two by John Peyton, Jr., because there is corroborating evidence from another member of the party. John Day, who was a servant in the Peyton household, confirms Slade's version of what happened. He said that the chief approached them with the bough of a tree in his hand, and that "he placed it on his forehead, *as a flag of truce*." (My italics.)

The chief's conduct was brave and dignified. When he tried to untie his wife's hands, the other men stopped him. The chief knocked two of them down with his fists and grabbed Mr. Peyton, Sr., by the collar and shook him violently. He believed that the senior Peyton was the leader of the party, and he was evidently trying to shake some sense into him. One of the crew stabbed him in the back and another shot him. John Day stated that the shooting and the stabbing occurred almost simultaneously. When the chief, despite his severe wounds, still held onto Peyton, Sr., the men moved in and beat him to death with the butts of their muskets.

John Day described the chief as a very tall man with a powerful physique. He remarked that the chief would have been a match for them all if they had not been armed.

From the eyewitness accounts of Slade and Day, it is clear

that the chief was not killed in self-defense as John Peyton, Jr., testified before the Grand Jury. Both men report that the chief approached them under a flag of truce, his manner was not threatening, and his only provocation was his attempt to rescue his wife. He did not use force until after he was stabbed in the back. As Slade states, "There was no necessity for the brutal act."

CHAPTER SEVEN

Mary March was Shananditti's aunt and the wife of a chief. Everyone who saw her agreed that she was a beautiful woman, with large black eyes set wide apart, high curving eyebrows, well-shaped nose and mouth, black hair, and a soft musical voice that delighted the ears. She was about twenty-four years old at the time of her capture. Her manners were very gentle and she showed great patience. Phrases such as "a gentle and interesting disposition" and "her whole demeanour agreeable" were used to describe her. Alert and inquisitive, she showed evidence of high intelligence. Beauty, patience, intelligence and gentleness—a rare combination of traits, a remarkable woman.

After her capture, Mary March stayed at the home of Reverend Leigh in Harbour Grace. During the next few months the Reverend had ample time to study her character and observe her habits. Almost a year after she left his house to return to her people, Mr. Leigh was visited by Sir Hercules Robinson, commander of H.M.S. *Favourite*, and asked to give a detailed description of her. A few weeks later Commander Robinson wrote down as many of the Reverend's comments as he could remember. This is the fullest portrait we have of Mary March.

"She was quite unlike an Esquimau in face and figure, tall and rather stout body, limbs very small and delicate, particularly her arms. Her hands and feet were very small and beautifully formed, and of these she was very proud, her complexion a light copper colour, became nearly as fair as an European's after a course of washing and absence from smoke, her hair was black, which she delighted to comb and oil, her eyes larger and more intelligent than those of an Esquimau, her teeth small, white and regular, her cheek bones rather high, but her countenance had a mild and pleasing expression. Her miniature taken by Lady Hamilton, is said to be strikingly like her; her voice was remarkably sweet, low and musical. When brought to Fogo, she was taken into the house of Mr Leigh, the missionary, where for some time she was ill at ease, and twice during the night attempted to escape to the woods, where she must have immediately perished in the snow. She was however carefully watched, and in a few weeks was tolerably reconciled to her situation and appeared to enjoy the comforts of civilization, particularly the clothes,—her own were of dressed deer-skins tastefully trimmed with martin, but she would never put them on, or part with them. She ate sparingly, disliked wine or spirits, was very fond of sleep, never getting up to breakfast before 9 o'clock. She lay rolled up in a ball in the middle of the bed. Her extreme personal delicacy and propriety were very remarkable and appeared more an innate feeling than any exhibition of 'tact' or conventional trick. Her power of mimicry was very remarkable and enabled her quickly to speak the language she heard, and before she could express herself, her signs and dumb Crambo were curiously significant. She described the servants, black-smiths, Taylor, shoemaker, a man who wore spectacles, and other persons whom she could not name, with a most happy minuteness of imitation; it is a beautiful provision that savages and children who have much to learn should be such good mimics, as without the faculty they could learn nothing, and we observe it usually leaves them when they no longer want its assistance. To this we should often ascribe family resemblances which we think are inherited, but to return to Mary March. She would sometimes though rarely speak fully to Mr Leigh, and talk of her tribe. They believed in a Great Spirit but seem to have no religious ceremonies—polygamy does not appear to be practiced. Mr Leigh is of opinion there are about 300 in number. I forget the data from which he calculated. They live in separate wigwams. Mary's consisted of 16—the number was discovered in rather a curious manner. She went frequently to her bed room during the day, and when Mr Leigh's housekeeper went up she always found her rolled in a ball apparently asleep. At last a quantity of blue cloth was missed, and from the great jealousy that Mary shewed about her trunk suspicion fell upon her. Her trunk was searched and the cloth found nicely converted into 16 pairs of moccasins, which she had made in her bed. Two pair of children's stockings were also found, made of a cotton night-cap. Mr Leigh had lost one, but Mary answered angrily about her merchandise 'John Peyton, John Peyton,' meaning he had given it to her; at last in the bottom of the trunk the tassell of the cap and the bit marked 'J.L.' were found. When looking steadfastly at Mr Leigh she pointed to her manufacture and said slowly—'Yours' and ran into the woods. When brought back she was very sulky and remained so for several weeks. The poor captive had two children and this was probably the tie that held her to her wigwam, for though she appeared to enjoy St. John's when she was taken there and her improved habits of life—she only 'dragged a lengthened chain' and all her hopes and acts appeared to have a reference to her return. She hoarded clothes, trinkets and anything that was given her and was fond of dividing them into 16 shares. She was very obstinate but was glad to be of any service in her power; if not asked to assist, she was playful, and was pleased with startling Mr Leigh by stealing behind softly. Her perception of anything ridiculous and her general knowledge of character showed much archness and sagacity. An unmarried man seemed an object of great ridicule to her. When she was taken into St. John's on entering the harbour, she said to Messrs. Leigh and Peyton, 'You go shore, John Peyton, when go shore no Emamoose,'(woman). She was quite indifferent to music, did not seem to perceive it, liked exhibiting herself to strangers, and was very fond of putting on and taking off all the dresses, ribbons and ornaments that were given her.

"Mr Leigh once drew on a bit of paper, a boat and crew, with a female figure in it going up a river and stopping a moment at a wigwam, described the boat freighted as before returning—Mary immediately applied the hieroglyphic, and cried out—'no,no,no,no.' She then altered the drawing taking the woman out and leaving her behind at the wigwam, when she cried very joyfully, 'Yes, Yes good for Mary.' "

This portrait of Mary March cannot be taken at face value. It tells as much about the biased nature of Sir Hercules Robinson as it does about the personality of Mary March. He views her with condescension, and sees her as a playful and sulking child who has not yet learned to appreciate the pleasures of music and the solemnity of religious ceremonies. He makes no effort to understand her cultural background and he shows no empathy for the problems and bewilderment of a captive held in a strange city and confronted by strange customs. He crassly assumes that she should be grateful to adopt his style of life and he is surprised to learn that she prefers to return to her life in the woods. In all his interpretations, Commander Robinson is mistaken; he is so convinced of the superiority of his own culture that he cannot see the existence of another.

It is a pity that there are no other portraits of Mary March, no other sources of information. The true source of her fascination will never be known.

Mary March remained with Reverend Leigh at his house on Twillingate Island for three months. During this time her progress in learning to speak English was so rapid that a number of people were encouraged in their belief that an effort should be made to open friendly communication with the rest of her people. With Mary's help the task would be much easier; the language barrier could be overcome. A great deal of faith was placed in the belief that Mary would tell her people about the good treatment she had received and convince them of the newly found good will of their former enemies.

The governor, Sir Charles Hamilton, ordered Captain William Nugent Glascock to proceed with haste in H.M.S. *Drake* to Twillingate Island and to pick up Reverend Leigh and Mary March. An invitation was sent to John Peyton, Jr., to join them, and he accepted.

By now the governor had some knowledge of the poor planning and bad judgement in the previous expeditions. He knew the risks involved and he was aware that an impulsive act or the hasty discharge of a firearm could jeopardize an entire expedition. He advised caution and restraint in his orders to the captain:

You will leave His Majesty's Sloop at Morton's Harbour and proceed with your boats, entering such bays and rivers as may be most likely to be frequented by the Indians during the summer season. But this is not to prevent you proceeding in the *Drake* to some other port further to the Northward if you can without unnecessary risk or hazard effect it with the assistance of any person acquainted with the coast. As the principal objects in view are to return the female Indian in question to her tribe and to establish a friendly communication with these aborigines, great care must be taken to select for this enterprise such persons of the crew as are most orderly and obedient, and every proper means you can suggest used to bring them to an interview, in doing which, as the greatest caution must be observed, it will be advisable to refrain from using fire-arms for any purpose before objects are accomplished.

As a further precaution the governor notified Captain Glascock of Peyton's involvement with the death of the Beothuck chief and the subsequent investigation of the Grand Jury:

I send herewith a Copy of the Proceedings on that occasion, together with the copy of Mr. Peyton's Narrative, and I desire that before leaving Morton's Harbour with the female Indian as directed by my order of this date, you do in conjunction with the Rev. Mr. Leigh (Magistrate) call before you the persons engaged in that expedition, and take down their examinations touching this transaction, and if it should appear that any of the party are culpable you are to bring him or them to St. John's to take their trial in the Supreme Court for the same, with such witnesses as may be necessary to establish the fact.

The governor, in asking Captain Glascock to obtain further testimony about the death of the Beothuck chief, was following the recommendations of the Grand Jury and acknowledging equal legal rights for all. Unfortunately there is no record of what Captain Glascock learned.

The expedition of Captain Glascock was well financed. No expense was spared to assure success, as shown in the following invoices of presents for the Beothucks which were loaded aboard H.M.S. *Drake*:

No. 1. List of Articles delivered to Captain Glascock of His Majesty's Sloop Drake for distribution among the Native Indians pursuant to the foregoing order—viz:

Blankets Double ....30 in No.
Frocks Red................................... 8 ″
Cloaks .... 5 ″
Looking-glasses, small........................24 ″
Knives...................................24 ″
Strings of Beads.............................15 ″
Dishes of Tin .... 3 sets of 6 Ea.
Small tin pots...............................12 in No.
Sail needles of sizes ....72 ″
Awls.................................24 ″

No. 2 List of Presents intended for the Native Indians.

   41 yds. Blanketing
17½ yds. Red Baize
    6 Single Hatchets
    1 Doz. Clasp Knives
    6 Boat's Kettles
    1 Doz. Men's Sanquahan Hose
    6 Teapots with covers
    6 tin Pints
    6 Hammers
    5 Pairs of Scissors
    1 Pair large ditto
    2 Doz. Iron tablespoons
    1 gross Middle G. Hooks
    2 Doz. Long Lines
    1 Doz. Rands of Sewing Twine
    3 tin Traps
    1 Pitsaw File
    1 Doz. Flat Files
    3 Tartan Caps
    4 Red Caps
  14 lbs. Soap
    6 Pairs of Child's Hose
    2 Lock Saws
    6 Tin Pans

```
  1 Tinder Box, complete
  1 Rand of Salmon Twine
  3 Doz. Trout Hooks fitted
400 Sewing Needles
  4 lbs. Bohea Tea
  6   "    Shingle Nails
 12   "    Mixed      "
  2   "    Thread of colours
  1 Iron Saucepan (gal)
  1   "        "   (quart)
 12 Pair of Blankets of Sizes
  2 Doz. Red Shirts
 30 lbs. Loaf Sugar
  1 Iron pot
9½ lbs. Cheese
  1 Doz. Rack Combs
  1 Oak Cask
  1 Cask Butter
```

Fort Townsend,
St. John's, Newfoundland.
3 June, 1819

Captain Glascock followed his orders with diligence and vigour. After picking up John Peyton and Mary March at Morton's Harbour on June 17, he sailed for Fortune Harbour and arrived there that evening. He decided that this port was the safest and most convenient place to anchor the H.M.S.*Drake*.

On the following day the captain and his crew proceeded in the cutter and the gig, accompanied by John Peyton and Mary March, to New Bay. After a lengthy search they found no signs that the Beothucks had visited that part of the coast in recent years. On the 22nd they proceeded in the cutter across The Bay of Exploits and up the river. During the night of the 24th they rowed with muffled oars and reached Bishop's Falls at dawn. Here they entered the woods and searched for recent campsites. Again they were disappointed. They returned down the river to the *Drake*, and on the 28th they repeated the journey up the River Exploits with muffled oars. Again disappointment. They travelled forty miles south to Indian Arm. Nothing. They travelled forty miles north to Badger Bay. Nothing. By now the crew was exhausted from rowing day and night, and their eyes were badly swollen from insect bites. Despite these hardships they refused to abandon the search.

On the 5th of July their luck changed. At Seal Bay, during a heavy thunder squall, they spotted a canoe a mile ahead of them. They gave chase and the canoe disappeared around a point of land. When they reached the point, the canoe was nowhere in sight. Captain Glascock guessed that the Beothucks had either sunk the canoe in deep water or carried it up the shore and into the woods. They landed and searched the woods, but could find no trace of the Beothucks or the canoe.

During this incident Mary March remained strangely quiet. Captain Glascock felt that she was indifferent to what was happening. He asked her if she wanted to follow the retreating Beothucks into the woods, or to remain with him. She preferred to stay.

The captain decided to leave Seal Bay that day and to return again in the night with the hope of surprising the Beothucks in the morning. This plan was followed, but nothing came of it.

In the following days the search was continued in the areas of Charles' Brook, the South Arm of New Bay, and Badger Bay. Nothing was found, and further effort seemed hopeless. Reluctantly the search was abandoned.

In his report to the governor, Captain Glascock concluded with these words:

Thus, Sir, have I accounted to you of the proceedings of the boats from 18th June to the 14th July, during which time a continual Night Guard has been rowed for upwards of ninety miles along the coast, and the most zealous and active energy manifested by the officers and ship's company I ever witnessed.

They have suffered much in consequence of being exposed for upwards of a week at a time in open boats, but custom would have seasoned them to this, could they have taken their natural rest by sleep, of which they were totally deprived by the tormenting tortures of every description of insects which infest this coast.

For his part in this strenuous search John Peyton, oddly enough, received high praise. Captain Glascock wrote the governor that he "could not have selected a more proper person to assist me in the execution of your orders." What prompted Peyton to serve so well? It is difficult to understand his motives, and the enigma of his character remains unexplained.

CHAPTER EIGHT

Mary March was returned to Reverend Leigh's house at Twillingate and new plans were made to unite her with her people. The knowledge that she was anxious to see her baby added sympathy for a hasty return. There was no way for Mary March to know that her baby was already dead. (It was learned later from Shananditti that the baby had died three days after the capture of its mother.)

Governor Sir Charles Hamilton decided that a new man was needed for the job, one with knowledge and previous experience in dealing with the Beothucks, a man of cool judgement who had strict control of his men. There was one man who met these qualifications better than anyone else—David Buchan. Since his assignment with the Beothucks eight years before, he had risen from lieutenant to commander.

The governor issued these orders to Buchan on August 8, 1819:

You are hereby required and directed to proceeed in His Majesty's Sloop Grasshopper under command to Twillingate, where you will deliver to the Rev. Mr. Leigh the accompanying letter respecting an Indian woman taken in the spring of this year, whose return to her tribe (the aborigines of this island) it is an object highly desirable to accomplish.

The governor had complete confidence in Buchan's ability: "It is entirely left to your discretion to adopt such course of proceeding as the information you will obtain may suggest."

When Commander Buchan arrived at Twillingate he was shocked to see Mary March in such poor health. It pained him to see her so thin and so poorly dressed. He immediately ordered warm dresses for her and arranged for a woman to care for her. In his judgement, her condition made travel impossible.

Buchan returned on November 25 and took Mary March aboard his ship, the *Grasshopper*. Here she remained for the next six weeks. It was Buchan's plan to wait until the River Exploits froze, then load her on a sleigh and take her up the river to the site where she was captured. He was certain her people would be in the area.

During this time aboard the *Grasshopper*, Mary's mood "always continued cheerful" although her health declined rapidly. She spoke frequently of her baby and took comfort in the belief that she would soon see him again. The crew was charmed by Mary's gentle grace and touched by her suffering.

That year the weather remained mild until the end of December and the river did not freeze as expected.

On January 8 Mary March was seized by a fit of suffocation. She called for Buchan and Peyton. They came to her side and she seemed to recover. Two hours later they left her, but were immediately summoned to return. They found her still and lifeless.

In his official report, Commander Buchan sent these words to the governor:

Her mild and gentle manners and great patience under much suffering endeared her to all, and her dissolution was deeply lamented by us.... the melancholy event had not been anticipated; it left me without instructions how to act, and as it was now out of my power to return to St. John's, I considered it still desirable to prosecute the original design, and many reasons determined me to have the corpse conveyed to the place of her former residence.

After ten months in captivity, Mary March was returning home—in a coffin.

With fifty men and supplies for forty days, Commander Buchan set out for the interior. Their destination was a hundred miles up the frozen river. The coffin containing

Mary's body was loaded on a sleigh and pulled by the men. In addition to their food and equipment, the men carried a large quantity of gifts for the Beothucks.

The journey was extremely difficult and the men suffered innumerable hardships. The ice on the river was treacherous and unstable. Sleighs shattered against blocks of ice, and feet were frozen from the cold water gushing through cracks. The entire party fell through the ice in one sudden collapse and many suffered frostbite as a result. Frequently the ice "burst with repeated noise, not unlike the discharge of Artillery." The men laboured with the burden of the coffin and the large quantity of gifts, but their spirits remained firm. Nothing could discourage them from returning Mary to her home.

At one spot on the river they found a thirty-foot raft and a large storehouse containing deer skins. A short way off they found a large quantity of venison hidden in the snow. From the foot prints and the disordered appearance of the site, it was evident that the Beothucks had left in a hurry. Buchan was certain that they had discovered the approach of his party and fled in terror. His hopes for a friendly interview were now greatly diminished. In his own mind, he was convinced that the capture of Mary March and the murder of the chief had been a tragic mistake, and that with Mary's death there was little hope of a reconciliation.

They reached the place where Mary March had been captured. "At three o'clock arrived at the former residence of our deceased friend. The frame of two wigwams remained entire, the third had been used as part of the materials in the erection of a cemetery of curious construction where lay the body no doubt of the Indian that had fallen, and with him all his worldly treasure, amongst other things was linen with Mr. Peyton's name on it, everything that had been disturbed was carefully replaced, and this sepulchre again closed up, some additional strengthening had been put to it this fall. The coffin which was conveyed to this spot with so much labour was unpacked and found uninjured, it was neatly made and handsomely covered with red cloth ornamented with copper trimmings and breastplate. The corpse, which was carefully secured and decorated with the many trinkets that had been presented to her, was in a most perfect state, and so little was the change in the features that imagination would fancy life not yet extinct. A neat tent that was brought for the purpose was pitched in the area of one of the wigwams, and the coffin covered with a brown cloth pall, was suspended six feet from the ground in a manner to prevent its receiving injury from any animals; in her cossack were placed all such articles as belonged to her that could not be contained in the coffin, the presents for the Indians were also deposited within the tent as well as the sledge on which they had been carried, and all properly secured from the weather."

Shananditti later reported that she had seen Commander Buchan and his party pass up the river with the coffin. She drew a sketch which showed the position of the Beothucks at the time and the route followed by Buchan. The sleighs used to pull the coffin and the gifts are clearly visible in the drawing (see opposite).

Shananditti's sketch is inscribed with these details:

The Indians were that winter encamped on the banks of the River Exploits, at A, and when they observed Capt. B. and party pass up the river on the ice, they went down to the seacoast near the mouth of the river, and remained a month; after that they returned up and saw the footprints of Capt. B.'s party, made on their return from the river, and to the spot where Mary March was left; which they reached in three days. They opened the coffin with hatchets, and took out the clothes etc. that were left with her; the coffin was allowed to remain suspended, as they found it, for one month; it was then placed on the ground, where it remained two months; when in the spring, they removed her into the cemetery they had built for her husband (who was unfortunately killed the year before) placing her at his side.

After ten months of separation, Mary March was united with her husband. Her capture had accomplished nothing but suffering and death.

Shananditti never told anyone in St. John's what she thought about the death of Mary March. Others have speculated that she looked upon it with some suspicion; she might have concluded that Mary died from poison, or some other foul means. If Shananditti had such thoughts, she can hardly be blamed for not commenting on Governor Hamilton's and Commander Buchan's muddle of good intentions.

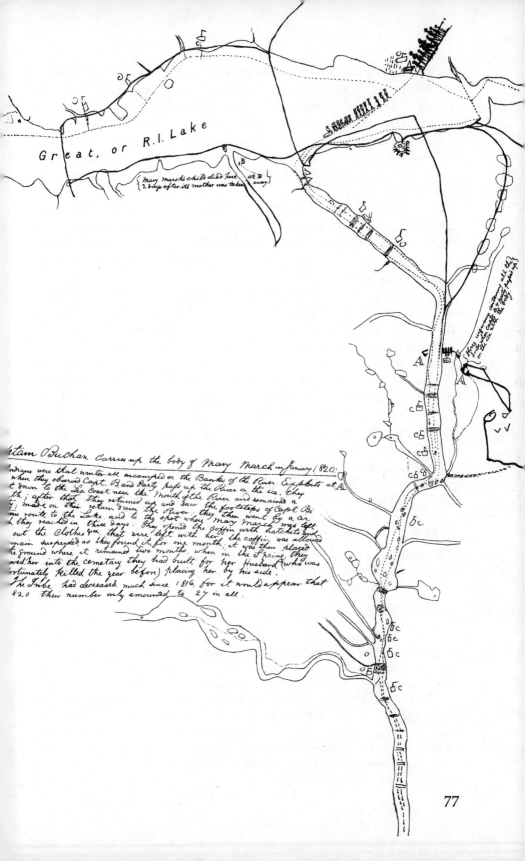

Great, or R.I. Lake

mary march's child died here   at B
2 days after its mother was taken away

B

A
A

tain Buchan carries up the body of Mary March in January 1820.

...ndians were that winter all encamped on the Banks of the River Exploits at A
...when they observed Capt. B and Party pass up the River on the ice, they
...t down to the Sea Coast near the Mouth of the River and remained a
...th; after that they returned up and saw the footsteps of Capt B:
...t; made on their return down the River, they then went by a ...
...ou route to the Lake and to the spot where mary march was left
...h they reached in three days. They opened the coffin with hatchets and
...out the Clothes &c. that were left with her, the coffin was allowed
...main suspended as they found it for one month; it was then placed
...he ground where it remained two months, when in the Spring, they
...wed her into the cemetary they had built for her Husband (who was
...fortunately killed the year before) placing her by his side.
...The Tribe had decreased much since 1816, for it would appear that
...820 their number only amounted to 27 in all.

Commander Buchan erred in taking Mary's body back to her people. For once in his remarkable career of clear-eyed command, he let sentiment cloud his judgement. The Beothucks could not see the return of her body as an act of sympathy, since they did not understand the reason for her capture in the first place. The only way they could make any sense of what had happened would be to view it as an outrageous insult.

Commander David Buchan's expedition was the last one commissioned by the governors of Newfoundland. All remaining attempts to contact the Beothucks were done by one individual, William Cormack, and each of his journeys ended in failure.

Thus ended government activity characterized by procrastination, ignorance, and ineptitude: not without good intentions, certainly, but abysmally lacking in good planning and understanding. Heroic efforts were made by a few individuals, but these were not enough. It was widespread prejudice and greed that pushed the Beothucks to extinction. To save them required the re-education of an entire population, but the leaders were not equipped for this. Rather the King's governors and magistrates were impatient to convert Newfoundland's "savages" to their way of life.

The last meeting between a party of Beothucks and a government official is typical of the rash judgement which all too often defeated the best of intentions. Captain J. Trivick was sailing the H.M.S. *Drake* in Badger Bay when he spotted three Beothucks paddling a canoe about one hundred and fifty yards away. Trivick was under strict orders from Captain Glascock not to fire at them. Here is Trivick's description of what happened:

I immediately made towards them endeavouring to make them understand that we wished to communicate with them, but they shewed no disposition to listen to us, were evidently getting away, and might if they got ashore easily escape into the woods, where it would be fruitless to follow them; under these circumstances I thought the only means left me to come up with them, was by firing a musket and thus throwing them into confusion, which it partially effected, but being by this time near the shore they unfortunately escaped as I anticipated.

I beg further to state that the almost certain hope of being able to intercept them before they got on shore, together with my anxiety and the utter impossibility of tracing them through the woods, could possibly have induced me so far to deviate from Capt. Glascock's orders not to fire.

We went into the woods after them, but found it in vain to pursue them; we left some presents in the wigwams near where the Indians landed, and afterwards pulled to some distance from this place and concealed ourselves in hopes of their returning but next morning when we went back we found everything in the state we left it; we came two days after and found they had returned and canoes, presents, etc., all taken away.

The Beothucks cannot be blamed for not trusting these overtures of "friendship." By this time they could only have seen Captain Trivick and his kind as a race of madmen.

CHAPTER NINE

The winter of 1822-23 was a hard one for Shananditti and her family. Most of their friends and relatives were now dead. Some had been shot for sport, some out of malice; some had been killed by trappers in abortive attempts to collect the government reward, and some had died from sickness and starvation.

Of the original population of seventy-two in the village when Shananditti was born, only twelve remained alive. These included her sister, her mother, her father, her uncle and her cousin. Before the end of the year, all these would be dead too, except Shananditti. A detailed sketch made by Shananditti records the tragic events during the winter and spring of 1823.

Shananditti was only twenty-two, but she had endured a lifetime of tragedy in a hostile environment. She had been shot and wounded; she had seen her uncle, Chief Nonos-bawsut, murdered; she had seen her aunt returned in a coffin, and had stood by helplessly while their baby died. She had seen disease and starvation pursue those who had escaped the trapper's bullet. She had seen babies die in the arms of mothers who could no longer provide them with nourishment. She had seen old men and women die because they refused food so that the younger ones might live. She had helped to bury the men, women and children of the village.

It was a cruel existence, and Shananditti could have no doubt about the ultimate end. There were no men left to marry, and no new babies would be born. She would never feel the affection of a man's arms around her, and she would never know the tenderness of a baby nursing at her breasts. She had known only the love of her family.

In March of 1823 the scarcity of food became so acute that Shananditti's uncle and cousin decided to travel to the coast, where food was more abundant. This was a dangerous decision, since they might be shot by one of many trappers and fishermen living there. Shananditti and her parents decided not to join them, so they proceeded by themselves.

Unarmed, weak from starvation, and exhausted from walking through the snow, they made their way towards Badger Bay. Their deerskin capotes and their sealskin boot-moccasins were torn and ragged. They were a pitiful sight and they could harm no one, but Curnew and Adams, the two fishermen who saw them, acted as if wild dogs were upon them. They shouted in alarm and ran for their muskets.

As the uncle walked towards them, his arms outstretched, begging for mercy and food, they shot him. As the cousin knelt in the snow and exposed her bare breasts to show that she was a woman, they shot her.

The same hunger that had driven the uncle and the cousin to the coast forced Shananditti and her mother and her sister to make the same journey. Her father, who had decided to hunt deer on his own, had not returned, and they feared that he was dead.

When the three women came upon the frozen bodies of the uncle and the cousin, they fled in panic. They travelled inland until they realized how futile it was, then they circled back to the shore in search of food.

What shock and anguish Shananditti must have felt when she came across the bodies of her uncle and cousin shot down under such pitiful circumstances. What kind of people were these murderers? In Shananditti's society it was unthinkable to kill a woman. The custom of baring the breasts under danger and duress was an ancient one. Shananditti believed that it was an inviolable symbol of woman's right to protection. Even the Vikings, who landed on the shores of Newfoundland long before the arrival of Cabot in 1497, had recognized this gesture of breast-baring and observed the sanction against killing women. Shananditti believed that the British must have no religion, no humanity. She often wondered how they treated their own women. In the Beothuck society, women had high value and enjoyed many special privileges.

As the three women searched the coastline, they were in desperate straits. Their supply of powdered eggs was gone, and they had no canoe to paddle out to one of the islands where the Great Auk laid its eggs. Their dried meat was gone, and they were incapable of killing a deer or a seal. They had no hooks and line, so they could not catch a salmon or cod. Food was all around them, but they could not get it.

For several weeks the three women lived on blue mussels which they pulled from the rocks along the ocean shore. There was nothing else to eat except the inner bark of trees and shrubs. There is very little nourishment in bark, but it did ease the pain of hunger somewhat.

They built a draughty hut from driftwood and camped near the windy shore. Their beaver mittens were worn out and their hands almost frozen; their fingers were so numb they could hardly hold the knife to open the shells. Each day they grew weaker and weaker, and they knew they could not live much longer on blue mussels and birch bark. Each day it became more and more evident that Shananditti's mother and sister had contracted some terrible disease, probably tuberculosis. Without better food and shelter, they would soon die.

They decided to give themselves up to the settlers. If they were shot, it was better than starving to death. And perhaps, just perhaps, they would meet some Englishmen with mercy in their hearts who would give them food and shelter.

There was really no other choice. They had to surrender. Their arms and legs were so thin they could see the contours of their bones. When they looked at each other, they saw living corpses.

They left the shore of Badger Bay and walked south along the river bank. It was a sunny day and the snow was beginning to melt. April is a welcome month in Newfoundland; it lifts the grey depression of the long, dull winter months. Unknown to the three women, it was the day before Easter.

The landscape in front of them was flat, etched with stubby pines growing in deformed wind-blown shapes. Here and there were large grey boulders, bare of snow, with brittle brown moss on the top and in the crevices. In the distance there were several small egg-shaped rocky hills, the glacial sculptures of a past ice age.

Through this desolate landscape the three women dragged themselves, frequently stopping to rest, then moving on with hunger-weakened steps. They expected to reach a settlement in two or three days. They did not expect to meet any one among the rocks and pines, but they were wrong. After four hours they came to a small gurgling creek, and there, squatting beside a half-skinned beaver, was a trapper whose face instantly froze their hopes of finding kindness. William Cull's ugly warts and red beard were a familiar and hated sight.

There is no record of Shananditti's thoughts on that fateful day in April. She may have prayed; she may have cried; she may have touched the good luck charm of seven lynx's teeth threaded on a cord which hung around her neck; she may have been too paralyzed with fear to move or respond. Certainly she must have hoped for a miracle to save her. And strange as it may seem, a miracle of sorts did occur.

Shananditti knelt in the snow. Her mother and sister knelt beside her. Death would be sudden. There was no time for words, no time to embrace and affirm their deep-felt love for one another. With their arms outstretched they pleaded silently for mercy.

Fifty yards across the snow, on the bank of a small creek with ice fringing both shores, the long black barrel of a musket was raised and aimed at them.

All three knew that Cull had murdered the mother's cousin twenty years before: shot her in the back while acting under the governor of Newfoundland's directive to return her to her village, and then stole the gifts the governor had given her in friendship. Now the same killer was facing them with his musket raised in hate. But something intervened to stop the cruel execution of these three innocent women. It was the basest of human motives: greed.

Shananditti knew nothing of the government reward for her capture and safekeeping. She had seen so many of her people killed by fishermen and trappers that she could not imagine that there were others living among them with kind hearts and humane motives.

As William Cull walked up to her, bringing the musket barrel towards the frightened face, she saw only savage glee in his eyes. She did not recognize the self-satisfaction of a man who was about to make a fast and easy profit. The reward of £100 sterling was worth several thousand dollars in today's equivalent value, and here were three helpless women passively offering themselves for his personal gain. He would collect three separate rewards. It was a lot easier than trapping beaver.

William Cull grabbed Shananditti by the arm and jerked her to her feet. He shoved her and motioned with his hand the direction he wanted her to go. He did the same with her mother and her sister.

Stunned by this inexplicable reprieve, Shananditti may have heard the words "St. John's" in the trapper's conversation with his companions, but she could not have recognized it as her destination. Nor could she even have guessed the strange way of life which lay ahead of her.

Cull pointed east towards the sea, put his musket on his shoulder, and walked in front of the three captives, who followed with grim resignation to whatever torture awaited them. They were convinced that their captors were delaying death only to make it more painful.

The party had travelled only a short distance along the bank of the creek when a shout in the woods to their rear caused them to stop and look back.

Through the bristling pines they could see a trapper in a red mackinaw running towards the creek. He was chasing someone and yelling for William Cull and his party to cut off the person who was fleeing.

Shananditti stared intently at the dark shadow of the man who was being chased. He was wearing a deerskin capote and there was something very familiar about this tall thin figure. Then she recognized the decorative fur trim on his coat. It was her father.

Shananditti was overjoyed and could not contain her excitement. When her father had not returned from hunting, she had thought he was dead. But there he was, running towards them through the pines, his clothes in rags.

When her father saw William Cull pointing a musket at him, he stopped quickly. There were trappers behind him, on his left, and in front of him. There was only one avenue of escape. He had no choice but to dash across the thin ice on the river.

There was no warning, no preliminary cracking noise, only a sudden splash of broken ice. Like a heavy brown stone, he sank beneath the surface.

The trappers ran to the bank and pointed their muskets at the hole in the ice, waiting for his head to reappear. A cloud of mud swirled in the water, a few bubbles floated to the surface, and all was silent. After several minutes the trappers lowered their weapons in disappointment.

That was the last time Shananditti saw her father.

CHAPTER TEN

William Cull's party and the three captive women travelled overland to a river leading into Badger Bay. How far and in what direction could not have mattered to Shananditti. The death of her father had left her in such despair that she was numb to what was happening. Her grief was reflected in the silent, starved faces of her mother and sister. They, too, were beyond caring.

The health of her sister was very poor. From time to time she would convulse with violent coughing. Tuberculosis had ravaged her lungs. Without medical care, she would not live long.

The mood of William Cull was entirely different. He was excited and boisterous, cursing with joy, full of plans about how he would spend the reward money. The other men shared his mood. This was the most excitement that they had seen in months, and maybe Cull would share some of the money with them.

As they approached the river the countryside took on a more fertile appearance. The trees grew taller and thicker. Between here and the River Exploits, they were suitable for lumber, and an active boatbuilding industry had sprung up. Trapping and boatbuilding were the winter work of the fishermen in Cull's party. Killing and bounty hunting were part of their recreation.

They loaded the women into a small boat and sailed down the river to the ocean. There they boarded a schooner and sailed towards the Bay of Exploits. This was the ancient habitat of the Beothucks. It was an ideal spot for settlement, now deserted. Its beauty was undisturbed by the new settlers. All the new arrivals lived on a number of islands some distance from the mouth of the river. These included Twillingate Island, Exploits Island, Burnt Island, and New World Island.

In 1823 the population of Twillingate was 720, and it was here that William Cull brought the three women. He gave them to John Peyton, Jr., who was the magistrate of the district.

Shananditti was delivered into the hands of one of the men who had murdered her uncle. However, instead of treating her cruelly, he conducted himself in a manner which indicated that he was personally concerned about her protection and well-being. He behaved as if he shared the governor's hope that the Beothucks could be saved from extinction.

The explanation of John Peyton's contradictory actions would seem to rest in the contrast between his duty as a judge and his nature as a man. He was an intensely materialistic person, not given to idealistic schemes, but his status obliged him to assist the governor in his declared aim to help the Beothucks.

Peyton took charge of the women and decided that it was best to take them to the governor in St. John's as soon as possible. Whether he felt that it was his responsibility to do this, or that he would gain favour with the governor, or simply that he wanted to get rid of them, is not known. Whatever his reasons, he loaded the three women aboard a new schooner recently christened *Ann*, and set sail for the seat of government in the new colony.

The voyage across two hundred miles of open sea was not easy. Although they were never out of sight of the coast, strong winds blew in from the Atlantic and storms were a common occurrence. It took courage, skill and toughness to travel in a small boat from Twillingate Island across Hamilton Sound, around Cape Freels, across Bonavista Bay, around Cape Bonavista, across Trinity Bay, around Grates Point, across Conception Bay, around Cape St. Francis and down the coast to St. John's.

A letter written by Commander David Buchan to the governor, Sir Charles Hamilton, revealed that on board the schooner was one of the two men (it is not known which,

Curnew or Adams) who had recently murdered Shananditti's uncle and cousin. Nothing is known about Peyton's role in the apprehension of this criminal, but it is apparent from the letter that Peyton had placed him under arrest and was taking him to St. John's to stand trial.

Some intriguing questions must go unanswered. Did Shananditti know that the murderer was aboard? What were her feelings? Did John Peyton know that the three women were related to the murdered man and girl? What were the murderer's thoughts and feelings?

The arrival of the three innocent captives on June 18 created a stir in St. John's. James Wheeler saw the women pass along the street and he gave this account: "The people stopped everywhere to look at them, especially the young folk, myself amongst the number, and when the children would crowd around them, Shanawdithit would make a pretence of trying to catch some of them. They would immediately scatter in all directions, child like, then she would give vent to unbridled laughter. Their fear appeared to be a matter which greatly pleased her, nor did she seem the least abashed at anything."

From the moment of his arrival, John Peyton was impatient. The governor was not there to meet him; what should be done? What about the health of the women? That same day he wrote a letter to Commander David Buchan, who he knew was well acquainted with the governor's scheme to establish friendly relations with the Beothucks, and whom he had met twelve years earlier around the time when Buchan's ill-fated expedition had made contact with the Beothucks. In view of this experience it was reasonable that Peyton would write to him for assistance:

Dear Sir,

I beg to inform you that I have now in my charge three women natives of this island who were taken in March and April last by Wm. Cull and others who consigned them to my care, being a Magistrate, and as I have reason to suppose that an amicable intercourse with these people is much desired by Government, I considered it best to bring them here in order to place them under the direction of His Excellency the Governor, but as I find that Sir Charles Hamilton is not yet arrived, I would most strenuously advise that they be immediately returned, and what renders this step most pressing is that one of them is far gone in a consumption, and the health of the other two has been very precarious since I have had them. That this object may be accomplished with the least possible delay I shall be happy to take them to the Bay of Exploits, whither I return immediately, and place them so near their people that they may readily rejoin them; and if this project meets your approbation, I would take the liberty of suggesting the propriety of providing such presents to be sent with them as will best promote the effect desired, and the cause of humanity.

As the schooner I brought them here in requires repair, it is desirable to provide them with a more eligible place of abode for the few days I remain at this place both on account of the general comfort of all, and the critical situation of the sick one who requires medical aid and attendance which can best be procured through your influence.

> I have the honour to be,
> Sir,
> Your most obedient, humble servant,
> (Signed) John Peyton, Jr., J.P.

Why did Peyton want to return immediately? The explanation he offers does not make sense. If one of the women was extremely ill, the return voyage would not improve her condition. Surely it was best to remain in St. John's where she could get rest and medical attention.

Commander Buchan sent an immediate reply to Peyton's letter. His concern for the welfare of the three women was genuine:

Sir,
Your letter of this day's date communicating the circumstances of your having brought with you three Native women of this Country, has been perused by me with much interest and consideration, and I hasten to acquaint you that Mr. Bland, the High Sheriff, is instructed to see that these objects of our solicitude be instantly provided with every requisite comfort suitable to their condition. Mr. Watt, Sur-

geon of the Grasshopper, [H.M.S. *Grasshopper* was an armed sloop under the command of David Buchan], will pay every attention in his power to promote the recovery of their health. The desirable object of endeavouring to open an amicable intercourse with their tribe shall have my fullest consideration.

I have the honour to be,
Sir,
Your most obedient, humble servant,
(Signed) D. Buchan, Comm.

There is no official record of what happened to the three women during their stay in the city, or what kind of medical attention they received. The only account we have is contained in the personal journal of a Methodist minister. The Reverend William Wilson had a sharp eye for detail, but a close examination of some parts of his journal reveals many factual errors. The following excerpt contains many fascinating details, but it is not entirely reliable:

June 23rd. The women were first taken to Government House and by order of his Excellency the Governor, a comfortable room in the Court House was assigned to them as a place of residence, where they were treated with every kindness. The mother is far advanced in life, but seems in good health. Beds were provided for them but they did not understand their use, and slept on their deer skins in the corner of the room. One of the daughters was ill, yet she would take no medicine. The doctor recommended Phlebotomy and a gentleman allowed a vein to be opened in his arm to show her that there was no intention to kill her, but this was to no purpose, for when she saw the lancet brought near her own arm, both she and her companions got into a state of fury; so that the Doctor had to desist. Her sister was in good health. She seemed about 22 years of age. If she had ever used red ochre about her person, there was no sign of it in her face. Her complexion was swarthy, not unlike the Micmacs; her features were handsome; she was a tall fine figure and stood nearly six feet high, and such a beautiful set of teeth, I do not know that I ever saw in a human head. She was bland, affable and affectionate. I showed her my watch, she put it to her ear and was amused with its tick. A gentleman put a looking glass before her and her grimaces were most extraordinary, but when a black lead pencil was put into her hand and a piece of white paper laid upon the table, she was in raptures. She made a few marks on the paper apparently to try the pencil; then in one flourish she drew a deer perfectly, and what is most surprising, she began at the tip of the tail. One person pointed to his fingers and counted ten; which she repeated in good English; but when she had numbered all her fingers, her English was exhausted, and her numeration if numeration it were was in Beothuck tongue. This person whose Indian name is Shanawdithit is thought to be the wife of the man who was shot. The old woman was morose, and had the look and action of a savage. She would sit all day on the floor with a deerskin shawl on, and looked with dread or hatred on every one that entered the Court house. When we came away, Shanandithit kissed all the company, shook hand with us and distinctly repeated good bye.

June 24th. Saw the three Indian women in the street. The ladies had dressed them in English garb, but over their dresses they all had on their, to them, indispensable deer-skin shawls; and Shanawdithit thinking the long front of her bonnet an unnecessary appendage had torn it off and in its place had decorated her forehead and arms with tinsel and coloured paper.

They took a few trinkets and a quantity of the fancy paper that is usually wrapped around pieces of linen; but their great selection was pots, kettles, hatchets, hammers, nails and other articles of ironmongery, with which they were loaded, so that they could scarcely walk. It was painful to see the sick woman who, notwithstanding her debility, was determined to have her share in these valuable treasures.

The man who was shot was Shananditti's uncle, not her husband. This was an understandable mistake, but it is strange that the Reverend should say that Shananditti was nearly six feet tall. All the other people who met her at this time or during the next six years agreed that she was much shorter, about five foot six. Perhaps being thin from starvation made her appear taller. All later accounts, however, support Reverend Wilson's description of her personality: she was affectionate, polite, and friendly. She had attractive features and beautiful teeth. She had a good memory, was eager to learn, and showed talent at drawing—all these suggest an alert, inquisitive person.

While the three women were promenading in St. John's,

Judge Peyton was busy with other matters. He collected, presumably on William Cull's behalf, the government reward of £100 for each Beothuck captive. It is not known if he obtained a commission for this service.

A trial was held for the man accused of killing Shananditti's uncle and cousin. John Peyton was undoubtedly present. It is unlikely that Shananditti was there, as there was no one who could translate for her. Commander Buchan wrote in a letter to the governor:

I also transmit for Your Excellency's information a copy of the legal proceedings taken relative to the murder of the two Indians. I trust that the measures taken by me in so important a crisis may meet with your approbation.

It would be instructive to see a copy of these proceedings and a transcript of the trial. All that is known is that the accused was acquitted; it was decided that there was no evidence against him.

Whatever his disappointment over the outcome of the trial, Commander Buchan did not let it dampen his spirits. He continued to take an active interest in the welfare of the three women. On June 28 he wrote to John Peyton, Jr., instructing him that the women "should be conducted with the least possible delay to such station as may enable them with the less difficulty to rejoin their tribe." He asked Peyton to leave a letter of instruction at various places where he could be found should the governor wish to communicate with him. "You will, therefore, again take charge of the three native females with the presents enumerated in the annexed schedule, which you will use as circumstances and your discretion may render most suitable as an incitement to these poor creatures to repose confidently in our people on that part of the coast they frequent." The safety and fate of the three women was again in Peyton's hands.

Shortly after receiving this letter Peyton sailed north, headed for the Bay of Exploits. He had decided to drop the women at Charles' Brook on the west side of the bay. Of the three women, only Shananditti would ever see St. John's again.

When they arrived at the Bay of Exploits, Peyton took the

women up the river and left them at the site of an abandoned Beothuck village. The absence of any signs of life in the area did not shake his confidence that the women would soon rejoin their friends and relatives. He gave them a small supply of food and gifts and returned to his island home.

Although Peyton was moved by a sense of duty rather than personal conviction, he did not neglect the three women. On July 23 he wrote to Commander Buchan:

Sir,
    I beg leave to acquaint you for the information of the Governor that I left the three Indian women on the 12th instant at Charles' Brook and that they appeared perfectly happy at our leaving them. I called there again on the 14th instant, when I gave them a little boat, at which the young woman was much pleased, and gave me to understand that she should go to look for the Indians and bring them down with her. [The young woman who expressed so much gratitude was, of course, Shananditti.] I am sorry to add the sick woman still remained without hopes of her recovery.

Peyton could not have known that the women had no chance of meeting any of their people, but he should not have left the three women alone, unprotected and with no shelter. Shananditti was the only healthy one; her mother was ill, and her sister dying. They had very little food and no skill or means for hunting. Much worse, they were in real danger: not from wild animals, but from man. If a fisherman or Micmac happened to come by and see them, they would probably be shot. Despite the enlightened views of the governor, a "shoot on sight" policy was still the general rule. It is hard to believe that Peyton could not see some of these dangers.

The mother and two daughters remained near the river, waiting for help. There was very little else they could do. Tuberculosis had a death grip on Shananditti's sister and made travel almost impossible. Shananditti was in good health, but she could not leave and search for help on her own, for it was now apparent that her mother was ill with the same terrible disease.

When their food ran out they were faced with starvation. It

94

was clear that they could not remain where they were. Their only hope was to return to the coast and beg food from the settlers.

How Shananditti managed to get the two sick women to the coast will never be known. Later she told Peyton that they walked down the right bank of the river. There is no record of what happened to the boat that Peyton had given them. Was it lost, stolen, damaged? It seems unlikely that Shananditti would have overlooked this easy form of transportation had it been available to them.

When they reached the coast, they came to one of Peyton's fishing stations. Here they received food and shelter. The pathetic sight of the sick and hungry women finally grazed the heart of John Peyton. He ordered some of his employees to build a "tilt house" on the shore of the bay not far from one of his own houses. This beach hut probably consisted of little more than a few poles and some canvas.

During this time Peyton witnessed an unusual medical practice. The mother attempted to cure her daughter by frequent steam baths. She heated some stones in a fire and dropped them into a pail of water inside the tilt house. She continued to do this until the little shelter was filled with dense steam. Then she uttered strange incantations, half songs, half shrieks. Peyton was astonished and a little taken aback by the mother's frenzy.

Needless to say, the steam treatment brought no improvement to the sick girl. Her condition grew steadily worse and she died in a few days.

Shananditti and her mother buried her in a strange way. They laid a sheet of birch bark on the ground and placed her on it. Then they covered her with another large sheet of bark and piled stones on top of this. What prayers were offered we do not know. The customary Beothuck funeral was an elaborate event, a ritual strikingly similar to ceremonies practised in ancient Egypt.

The mother's health declined rapidly after the death of her daughter, and she died a week later. There is no mention of her burial, but it is probable that Shananditti followed the same ceremony given her sister.

Shananditti, child of sorrow, was now alone. She got into a small flat boat and paddled many miles across the bay to

Burnt Island, where John Peyton maintained a permanent residence and employed a fair number of servants and staff.

CHAPTER ELEVEN

With her mother and sister gone, there was no one to share Shananditti's grief, no one to talk with her, no one to comfort her. She was the last Beothuck, totally alone.

Yet Shananditti was able to face her isolation with remarkable strength. Rather than yielding to bitterness or sorrow she entered the Peyton household, shared in the daily chores, and began to learn English. Because the Peytons did not know her Beothuck name, they gave her another: Nancy April, after the month in which she had been captured. (Her sister had been referred to as Easter Eve, after the day of the capture, and her mother had been called Betty Decker because William Cull and his party, in addition to trapping, were engaged in decking a boat at the time.)

Occasionally Shananditti was overwhelmed by the painful memories of her past; she gave in to moods of gloom, and ceased all activity. When this happened, she performed an amazing cure. Perhaps this was the secret of her strength and courage. Mrs. Gill, a servant in the Peyton household, told what happened. "At times she fell into a melancholy mood, and would go off into the woods, as she would say to have a talk with her mother and sister. She generally came back singing and laughing, or talking aloud to herself. She would frequently indulge in the same practice at night, and when asked what was the matter would reply, '[Shananditti] talking to her mother and sister.' When told not to be foolish, that they were dead and she could not talk to them, she would say, 'a yes they here, me see them and talk to them.'"

If this habit of talking to her dead mother and sister gave

her the strength and courage to go on living, it can hardly be called foolish. The actual rite remains a mystery, but evidently it restored her spirits and enabled her to perform daily routine tasks cheerfully. It was an extraordinary thing.

From all accounts, Shananditti was a good worker. Mr. Curtis, a friend of the Peytons, was impressed with her diligence: "Whilst she lived with Peyton she acted freely and without being obliged, the part of servant, and a very industrious and intelligent servant she was. She made the fire, prepared the tea, swept and scrubbed the floor, washed the clothes, cooked, etc. She never made the bread. I never saw her with a needle, but I often saw her stitch by passing the thread through a hole made with a sharp point or awl." A servant who worked with Shananditti said that she was "a fine worker, was a good clean cook and washer."

Shananditti was a servant, but she was never servile. She maintained a will of her own, as shown by the comments of Mrs. Gill: "Nance [Shananditti] was very pert at times and openly defied Mrs. Peyton when the old lady happened to be cross with the servants. Nance would laugh in her face, and say, 'well done Misses, I like to hear you jaw, that right'; or 'jawing again Misses.' " Mrs. Jure, who was also a servant at the Peytons', confirmed this. She said that Shananditti "was bright and intelligent, quick to acquire the English language, and of a retentive memory. She was very pert at times, and when her mistress had occasion to scold her, she would answer very sharply, 'what de matter now Missa Peyton, what you grumble bout.' "

The children in the Peyton house soon grew very attached to Shananditti. Bishop Englis, a visitor from Nova Scotia, was struck by the demonstrative display of affection. He wrote that "She is fond of children, who leave their mother to go to her."

The women in the Peyton house were impressed with Shananditti's conduct with men. Mrs. Gill said that "She was strictly modest and would allow no freedom on the part of the opposite sex. Once when an individual attempted some familiarity he was so rudely repulsed that he never afterwards dared to repeat the offence. She would not tolerate him near her. He was a Mudty man (bad man). She seemed well aware of the difference between right and wrong, and knew if a person cursed or swore he was doing wrong; 'mudty man' she would say."

Shananditti was not, however, prudish or fearful of all men. One day she surprised Mrs. Jure with an amusing display of affection for a shy man. "She would allow no familiarity on the part of the fishermen who frequented Peyton's house, but on one occasion, when amongst others, an individual possessing an extremely red beard and hair was amongst the number, she showed the greatest partiality to this man, even going to the length of sitting on his knee and caressing him; to the no small confusion of the big shy fisherman and to the great amusement of his companions."

The red hair of the big shy fisherman must have been part of his attraction, since Shananditti held the colour red in very high esteem. The shyness of the man might have appealed to her, too, since so many aggressive males had passed through her life.

Busy as she was, not all of Shananditti's time was taken up with work. She spent many hours drawing and carving. Mrs. Gill said that "She was very gentle and not at all of a vicious disposition, was an adept at drawing or copying anything. Capt. Buchan took her on board his man-of-war, gave her drawing paper and materials etc., he then showed her a portrait of his mother which she copied very accurately. She made very neat combs out of deers horns and carved them all over elaborately. She would take a piece of birch bark, fold it up, and with her teeth bite out various designs representing leaves, flowers, etc. Her teeth were very white and even." Mrs. Jure confirmed this: "She was very ingenious at carving and could make combs out of deers' horns and carve them

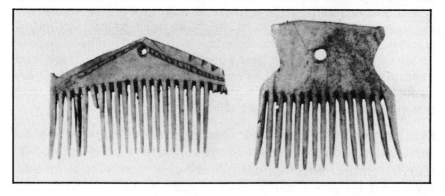

beautifully. She would take a piece of birch bark, double it up and bite with her teeth into a variety of figures of animals or other designs, i.e. to say when the bark was again unfolded, the impressions thereon would be such."

Like women the world over, Shananditti was interested in clothes. Mrs. Gill said that "She was fond of colours and fine clothes. Capt. Buchan sent her a pair of silk stockings and shoes from St. John's in which she took great pride."

When Bishop Englis visited Mr. Peyton on July 2, 1827, he spoke with Shananditti and wrote this interesting description of her which later appeared in the *Annals of the Society for the Propagation of the Gospel for 1856*.

Her progress in the English language has been slow, and I greatly lamented to find that she had not received sufficient instruction to be baptised and confirmed. I should have brought her to Halifax for this purpose but her presence will be of infinite importance if any more of her tribe should be discovered. She is now 23 years old, very interesting, rather graceful, and of a good disposition; her countenance mild, her voice soft and harmonious. Sometimes a little sulkiness appears, and an anxiety to wander, when she will pass twenty four hours in the woods, and return; but this seldom occurs.

The bishop was mistaken about her age, and about a few other matters as well.

During the bishop's visit a congregation was assembled on Burnt Island and forty-nine persons were confirmed. Shananditti was present and she watched the proceedings with interest. Bishop Englis wrote that

She perfectly understood that we were engaged in religious services, and seemed struck with their solemnity. Her whole deportment was serious and becoming. She was also made to understand my regret that her previous instruction had not been such as to allow of her baptism and confirmation, and my hope and expectation that she would be well prepared, if it should please God that we meet again. Mr. Peyton pledged himself that every possible endeavour should be made for this purpose.

Mr. Peyton was more polite than truthful. It appears that he made no attempt to prepare Shananditti for Christianity. Mr. Curtis remarked that "Peyton's religion was very unobtrusive, and he never had prayer in common in his house, in which Nance might join. I am unable to say whether she or the others were baptised, certainly they showed no knowledge of christianity."

While Shananditti was with the Peytons there was one visitor who filled her with terror. He was a Micmac named Noel Boss. Shananditti called him Mudty Noel (Bad Noel). Whenever he appeared, she would run screaming to Mr. Peyton and cling to him for protection. Even the sight of Boss's dog filled her with dread.

When the Peyton household inquired about her fear of Noel Boss she said that he had shot at her across a river as she was stooping to clean some venison. His shots had hit her in the hand and the leg. She had dropped the venison and run limping into the woods. As she described the frightening incident, she limped about the room acting out the scene. In proof of her story, she showed the scars of the gunshot wounds.

Mrs. Gill told her son that Noel Boss "boasted of having killed 99 Red Indians in his time, and wished to add one more to the number so as to complete the hundred. He afterwards fell through the ice on Gander Lake while laden with six heavy steel traps, and was drowned, by far too good a fate for such a monster."

There was another notorious Beothuck killer living nearby. His name was Mr. Rogers. This description of him appeared in a letter to the editor in the *Liverpool Mercury*, written by E. Slade, a friend of Mr. Peyton: "I have heard an old man named Rogers living on Twillingate Great Island boast that he had shot at different periods above sixty of them. So late as 1817, this wretch accompanied by three others one day discovered nine unfortunate Indians lying asleep on a small island far up the bay. Loading their guns very heavily, they rowed up to them and each taking aim fired. One only rose, and rushing into the water endeavoured to swim to another island, close by, covered with wood: but the merciless wretch followed in the boat, and butchered the poor creature in the water with an axe, then took the body to the shore and piled it on those of the other eight, whom his companions had in the meantime put out of their misery. He minutely described to me the spot, and I afterwards visited the place, and found their bones in a heap, bleached and whitened with the winters blast." It is not known that Shananditti ever met Mr. Rogers, but in such a small community it is hard to believe that she did not occasionally see him.

The presence of these vicious Indian killers in the vicinity must have preyed on Shananditti's peace of mind, but there is no evidence that these two men threatened her safety.

CHAPTER TWELVE

For five years Shananditti remained in the Peyton household. For five years she lived in the obscurity of Burnt Island near the Bay of Exploits. No one recognized her unique importance as the sole survivor of an ancient culture, the only source of invaluable information which would be lost forever when she died.

Did Shananditti survive starvation, disease, attempted murder, bounty-hunters, massacres, and misguided government policies only to die with the secrets of the Beothuck culture? Fortunately not. During the last year of her life, William Cormack, a philanthropist and world traveller, "discovered" her.

William Epps Cormack was one of those daring persons who forsake the security of a regular job and place of residence to seek new lands and dangerous enterprises. A man of action and brains, an innovator and an organizer, an explorer and a philanthropist, he had been born in St. John's, May 5, 1796 to Scottish parents. His father, who was a well-to-do merchant, gave him a liberal education. At the University of Edinburgh, "under the tuition of Prof. Jameson," he acquired a good practical knowledge of the sciences, especially botany, geology and mineralogy. Whether this education unfitted him for commercial pursuits, or whether his natural inclinations tended towards a more cosmopolitan existence, he became a world traveller whose journeys usually had a philanthropic side, such as the collection of information to establish an agricultural society, a fishing industry, or a tobacco plantation.

In 1822, when Cormack became the first European to cross the interior of Newfoundland, his aim was to bring about friendship with the Beothucks. He was filled with a deep sympathy for these persecuted people. As one observer said, "He threw himself, heart and soul into this cherished idea, nor did he count the risks and dangers that confronted him in the least. The one desire of his life so actuated him that he seemed to look upon himself as the instrument by which the amelioration of the condition of the Beothuck was to be accomplished."

On October 2, 1827, William Cormack stood up in the Court House at Twillingate and gave an impassioned speech to a distinguished audience which included the senior assistant judge of the Supreme Court, the judge of the North Circuit Court, Doctor Tremlet, and the Reverend John Chapman. John Peyton, Jr., was among those who listened to Cormack's spirited message. Since the words reveal the man, and account for so much that happened later, it is worth quoting this speech in full:

Every man who has common regard for the welfare of his fellow beings, and who hears of the cause for which we are now met, will assuredly foster any measures that may be devised to bring within the protection of civilization that neglected and persecuted tribe—the Red Indians of Newfoundland. Every man will join us, except he be callous to the misfortunes or regardless of the prosperity of his fellow creatures. Those who by their own merits, or by the instrumentality of others, become invested with power and influence in society, are bound the more to exert themselves—to do all the good they can, in promoting the happiness of their fellow men: and if there be such men in Newfoundland, who say there is no good to be gained by reclaiming the aborigines from their present hapless condition, let them not expose their unvirtuous sentiments to the censure of this enlightened age. Is there no honest pride in him who protects man from the shafts of injustice?—nay, is there not an inward monitor approving of all our acts which shall have the tendency to lessen crime and prevent murder?

We now stand on the nearest part of the New World to Europe—of Newfoundland to Britain; and at this day, on this sacred spot, do we form the first assembly that has ever yet collected together to consider the condition of the invaded and ill-treated first occupiers of the country. Britons have trespassed here to be a blight and a scourge to a portion of the human race; under their (in other respects) protecting powers, a defenceless, and once independent, proud tribe of men, have been nearly extirpated from the face of the earth—scarcely causing an enquiry how, or why. Near this spot is known to remain in all his primitive rudeness, clothed in skins, and with a bow and arrow only to gain his subsistence by, and to repel the attacks of his lawless and reckless foes: there on the opposite approximating point, is man improved and powerful:—Barbarity and civilization are this day called upon to shake hands.

The history of the original inhabitants of Newfoundland, called by themselves Beothuck, and by Europeans, the Red Indians, can only be gleaned from tradition, and that chiefly among the Micmacs. It would appear that about a century and a half ago, this tribe was numerous and powerful—like their neighboring tribe, the Micmacs:—both tribes were then on friendly terms, and inhabited the western shores of Newfoundland, in common with the other parts of the Island, as well as Labrador. A misunderstanding with the Europeans (French) who then held the sway over those parts, led, in the result, to hostilities between the two tribes; and the sequel of the tale runs as follows.

The European authorities, who we may suppose were not over scrupulous in dealing out equity in those days, offered a reward for the persons or heads of certain Red Indians. Some of the Micmacs were tempted by the reward, and took off the heads of two of them. Before the heads were delivered for the award, they were by accident discovered, concealed in the canoe that was to convey them, and recognized by some of the Red Indians as the heads of their friends. The Red Indians gave no intimation of their discovery to the perpretrators of the unprovoked outrage, but consulted amongst themselves, and determined on having revenge. They invited the Micmacs to a great feast, and arranged their guests in such order that every Beothuck had a Micmac by his side, at a preconcerted signal each Beothuck slew his guest. They then retired quickly from those parts bordering on the Micmac country. War of course ensued. Firearms were little known to the Indians at this time, but they soon came into more general use amongst such tribes as continued to hold intercourse with Europeans. This circumstance gave the Micmacs an undisputed ascendancy over the Beothucks, who were forced to betake themselves to the recesses of the Interior, and retired parts of the island, alarmed, as well they might be, at every report of the fire-lock.

Since that day European weapons have been directed, from every quarter, (and in latter times too often) at the open breasts and unstrung bows of the unoffending Beothucks. Sometimes these unsullied people of the chase have been destroyed wantonly, because they have been thought more fleet, and more evasive, than men ought to be. At other times, at the sight of them, the terror of the ignorant European has goaded him on to murder the innocent,—at the bare mention of which civilization ought to weep. Incessant and ruthless persecution, continued from many generations, has given these sylvan people an utter disregard and abhorrence of the very signs of civilization. Shawnawdithit, the surviving female of those who were captured four years ago, by some fishermen, will not now return to her tribe, for fear they should put her to death; a proof of the estimation in which we are held by that persecuted people.

The situation of the unfortunate Beothuck carries with it our warmest sympathy and loudly calls on us all to do something for the sake of humanity. For my own satisfaction, I have for a time, released myself from all other avocations, and am here now, on my way to visit that part of the country which the surviving remnant of the tribe have of late years frequented, to endeavour to force a friendly interview with some of them, before they are entirely annihilated: but it will most probably require many such interviews, and some years, to reconcile them to the approaches of civilized man.

Several gentlemen of rank, in England and elsewhere, have viewed with regret the cruelties that have been exercised towards these people; and have offered to come forward in support of any measures that might be adopted, to offer them the protection and kindness of civilization. Amongst the foremost of those are His Lordship the Bishop of Nova Scotia — and amongst ourselves, the Hon. Augustus Wallet Des Barres. I lay his Lordship the Bishop's correspondence upon that subject on the table. After this day we shall expect the co-operation of many such independent and enlightened men.

I hope to be able to effect, in part, the first objects of the Institution — that of bringing about a reconciliation of the Aborigines, to the approaches of civilization. I have already commenced my measures, and am determined to follow up, in progression, what steps may appear to the best for the accomplishment of the object I have long had in view. I hope to state to the public, in a few weeks, the result of my present excursion; on which I am to be accompanied by a small party of other tribes of Indians.

Cormack's rhetoric and persuasion were well suited to the occasion, and his conviction touched all those present. Following this speech twenty-two resolutions were proposed, and all of them were passed unanimously. Among these were the following, as recorded in the minutes of the meeting:

It was then proposed by W.E. Cormack, Esq.— seconded by Charles Simms Esq. and unanimously resolved,—That a Society be formed to be called the"Boeothick Institution," for the purpose of opening a communication with, and promoting the civilization of the Red Indians of Newfoundland.

2ND.—Proposed by Joseph Simms, Esq.— seconded by John Stark, Esq., and unanimously resolved,—That this Institution shall be supported by voluntary subscriptions and donations; and that persons be appointed at different places to receive the same.

7TH.—Proposed by the Reverend John Chapman,—seconded by Thomas Slade, Esq.—and unanimously Resolved,—That W.E. Cormack Esq. be President and Treasurer.

15TH.—Proposed by Thomas Lyte, Esq.—seconded by the Reverend John Chapman— and unanimously Resolved,—That Shawnawdithit be placed under the paternal care of the Institution; the expense of her support and education to be provided for out of the general funds.

16TH.—Proposed by Doctor Tremlet—seconded by Thomas Lyte, Esq.—and unanimously Resolved,—That the best thanks of this meeting are due, and hereby given to W.E. Cormack, Esq. the founder of this Institution, for the deep concern and great interest he has already taken in attempting a communication with the Red Indians, in his perilous journey across this Island, in the year 1822; and for his praiseworthy perseverance to establish, on a solid basis, the means of attaining the objects of this Institution.

Thus, in a very short time, William Cormack accomplished what all before him had failed to do. He drew public attention to the Beothucks; he aroused the moral indignation of others "to do something for the sake of humanity"; he formed a society for the preservation of the Beothucks; he brought recognition of the unique value of Shananditti, and he launched a program of investigation into the Beothuck culture. As the founder of the Beothuck Institution, Cormack could be justly proud.

Cormack had strong hopes of contacting the Beothuck culture's "surviving remnant" which he believed existed in some "sequestered spot" of Newfoundland. With funds from the Beothuck Institution he hired three Indians the following spring to search for the remaining Beothucks. Their names were John Louis, John Stevens, and Peter John. For some reason Cormack did not accompany the three. He wrote them a detailed set of instructions of where to look, and he offered them a bonus of £100 if they discovered any living Beothucks.

In his list of instructions Cormack wrote that his three explorers must "at all times bear in mind that great caution and perseverance are eminently requisite to accomplish the important and intricate designs of the Institution, and they will avoid coming in contact with the Red Indians under any circumstances however favorable they may appear to be." He instructed them "to ascertain as correctly as they possibly can the numbers of the Red Indians now in existence and the country occupied by them, and they will then immediately return to St. John's to report the particulars of their discovery in order that another expedition upon a more matured plan, and other measures, expedient and necessary may be adopted by the Institution."

The party left on February 12, 1828, and they were in good spirits. Cormack received word that "they seem to be almost confident of finding them."

Disappointment followed disappointment. Despite a difficult four months search, paddling up and down rivers

108

and combing the shores of lakes and bays, the three Indians could find no trace of any living Beothuck.

On June 21 Cormack wrote to his friend, John Stark, and informed him of the sad news. However, he was still not ready to abandon hope:

My dear Stark,

The three Indians John Louis, John Stevens and Peter John returned here last night, in a schooner from river Exploits. They travelled from Bay of Despair to St. George's Bay (harbour)—thence W.70 N. to Bay of Islands—over the Bay of Islands Lake—thence S.E. to the Red Indian Lake, and down the River Exploits: the only place left unsearched (and that above all others where they are most likely to be found) is White Bay. They ought to have gone there before they returned. We think of sending them now, in a vessel going that way, to White Bay and settle the question as speedily as possible, whether any of the Boeothucks survive or not. This vessel goes hence on Tuesday. We are to have a consultation to day.

I remain my dear Sir,
Yours very truly,
(Signed) W.E. Cormack

At a meeting of the Beothuck Institution three days later it was decided unanimously "That the three Indians be again employed to proceed forthwith to explore and examine the country in the interior of and adjacent to White Bay: and the President of the Institution be authorized to employ one of the European settlers to accompany the Indians."

In his methodical manner Cormack wrote another set of instructions. He implored the men to be "careful to examine particularly the whole of the lakes, rivers and country along the route now described, so that the party may be able to give the most unequivocal information that no part of the country has been left unsearched." He asked John Louis, the leader of the expedition, to make a map, "marking down every lake, river and mountain, so that Mr. Peyton who is already intimately acquainted with the interior may be able to afford the Institution his opinion and observations thereon."

109

As an incentive for the searchers to put forth every effort, Cormack increased the bonus. This time the men would receive £150, a considerable sum in those days, if they located a living Beothuck. They found none.

CHAPTER THIRTEEN

With much diminished prospects of ever finding another Beothuck, William Cormack turned his attention to Shananditti. Cormack had remarked to a group of friends that "It appears extraordinary, and it is to be regretted, that this woman has not been taken care of, nor noticed before, in a manner which the peculiar and interesting circumstances connected with her tribe and herself would have led us to expect." He was critical of the indifference of government officials, and their failure to provide Shananditti with some kind of protection. In a letter to the Bishop of Nova Scotia, Cormack wrote that "It is a melancholy reflection that our Local Government has been such as that under it the extirpation of a whole Tribe of primitive fellow creatures has taken place. The Government and those whose dependence on it overcame their better feelings still withhold their countenance from the objects of the Institution, and protection from the unfortunate female dropped off among us from the brink of the extermination of her tribe." He was anxious to enlist the aid of responsible people for her safety and education. At the end of his letter to the Bishop, he added these remarks: "Looking forward, I entreat you to learn from time to time how she is coming on; for it is to such feelings as yours and Mr. Simms' that this unprotected creature will owe her value, and be prevented from sinking into abject dependance. She is already a faithful domestic servant. I say these things merely from the fear that she might be cast on the mercy of the Local Government of N.F.L. [Newfoundland], under which all the rest of the tribe have suffered."

An uneasy feeling of urgency now came over him. If something should happen to Shananditti, the secrets of the Beothucks would be lost forever. Both his concern for her safety and his curiosity about her ancient culture and the history of their last years were intense.

It was decided at a meeting of the Beothuck Institution "That the instruction of Shawnawdithit would be much accelerated by bringing her to St. John's." In all likelihood it was Cormack who urged this motion, but others were thinking the same thing, as shown in this extract from a letter which John Stark wrote to Cormack on September 12, 1828:

The more I thought of her deplorable and dark situation, the more I have been impressed with the great importance of her education being proceeded in forthwith. In addition to every other consideration, I feel that individually and collectively the Boeothuck Institution are doubly called upon to take that unfortunate creature under our own immediate protection, for shall it be said that we have held out to the public hopes which cannot be realized, or shall we permit ourselves to be accused of lukewarmness in a cause likely to be so glorious in the results, nay but setting aside these propositions, shall we not as members of society do all in our power to reclaim these propositions, shall we not as members of society do all in our power to reclaim a very savage from the verge of continued ignorance. I am sure you will heartily join with me in the opinion I have now expressed of her speedy removal to St. John's not only as a measure calculated to do her a real service, but a measure which will afford you and me the satisfaction of knowing that we have contributed our mite in the general cause of humanity.

Four days later John Stark wrote Cormack from Twillingate to inform him that Shananditti would sail for St. John's at eight o'clock the next morning. He offered Cormack, who was a bachelor, some curious advice:

Let me suggest that a stout watch should always be kept over her morals and that no one should be allowed to see her without special permission. You will I dare say tell me it is in vain for me to suggest these things to a man of your sound sense and discriminating knowledge of human nature, yet I feel that if I were to neglect doing so, I might perhaps blame myself when it would be too late. The great interest taken in this unfortunate creature by the Attorney General renders him peculiarly well fitted, being a married man, to advise you what to do upon the occasion.

Mr. Stark's advice is very touching, but it shows that he had no knowledge of Shananditti's strong moral character. Perhaps he was worried about the reaction of the public when it became known that an attractive young woman was living in the house of an adventuresome bachelor.

The question of Cormack's marital status came up again in an odd way. As Shananditti was about to step on board the schooner for the long sea voyage to St. John's, John Stark handed her a letter to deliver to Cormack. It read:

Dear Cormack,
This note will I trust be handed to you by the Red Indian Shawnawdithit herself. She asked me if you had any family, I told her that when I left St. John's you were single but that I could not tell how long you would remain so. Above all things I request you will get her vaccinated by Doctor Carson upon the very day she reaches St. John's, pray let nothing prevent this.

Yours faithfully,
(Signed) John Stark

We must not be tempted to read too much into John Stark's words, but there is another remark in his previous letter which seems to hint at some problem: "I ought to say that Mrs. Peyton was quite willing for her to come away and I hope Mr. Peyton will not be displeased." Shananditti was a good worker and the Peytons were losing the benefit of her services, but maybe there was some substance to the earlier comment that the Peyton children were more fond of Shananditti than they were of their own mother.

The precaution of having Shananditti vaccinated against smallpox was good advice. But it was too late. When she arrived in St. John's to start a new life, she was already infected with tuberculosis, the terrible disease that had killed so many of her people whenever they came in contact with Europeans. Shananditti was certainly familiar with the symptoms of the disease, and she had, no doubt, realized her fate some time before the others recognized it.

Shananditti's second visit to St. John's was accompanied by even more interest and excitement than her first. The public were well informed through the newspapers of her arrival. This striking announcement appeared in the October 21 issue of the *Royal Gazette*:

Those who are curious in enquiries relating to man have a treat just now in St John's such as is not likely again to be met with. There are at present at Mr Cormack's house, accessible at all times to those who feel an interest, individuals belonging to three different tribes of North American Indians, viz. a Mountaineer from Labrador,—two of the Banakee nation from Canada,—and a Boeothick, or Red Indian of Newfoundland, the last a female. They all speak different languages—and are good specimens of the race. The men are 5 feet 10 inches and a 1/2 and 5 feet 11 inches in height.

The three men are, those that were sent a few months ago, in search of the Red Indians. They have returned without finding any recent traces of these people to the North or in the vicinity of White Bay.

The Bishop of Nova Scotia sent William Cormack a letter of congratulations. The bishop declared that he was "glad that poor Shawnawdithit is in such good hands, where due regard will I trust be given her moral and religious instruction." Although the two men were good friends, Cormack did not comply with this request. This was the second time that Bishop Englis had asked someone to give religious instruction to Shananditti and it was the second time that his request was ignored. In Cormack's case the bishop had things backwards. Cormack wanted Shananditti to instruct him in her religion.

It seems unlikely that Cormack would have made Shananditti as accessible to the public as the newspaper article indicated. She was a treasure far too valuable to parade as a public curiosity. He had, however, solicited public contributions for her support and for his expenses, so perhaps a measure of public attention was necessary.

It is a pity that there is so little information about what actually happened, no record of Shananditti's feelings and thoughts during this strange time in her life. We can surmise from the scattered comments of others that she was happy with the attention Cormack was giving her and eager to work on the project he had set for her. But what did she think of the crowded city with strange buildings where the customs, commerce, and people were so different from those she had grown up with? There is no doubt that living with the Peytons in the small settlement at Exploits provided an introduction and a preparation for what would otherwise have been a paralyzing dose of culture shock.

CHAPTER FOURTEEN

Shortly after Shananditti arrived in William Cormack's household, the president of the Beothuck Institution embarked on a last search for her tribesmen, a journey that would take him two hundred miles in thirty days. Although strong and well-equipped, Cormack was not prepared for the hardships and disappointments which lay ahead. A friend of John Peyton, Jr., later wrote this comment: " Mr. Peyton informed me that he saw Cormack before he entered upon this journey, that he was a lithe, active, robust man. When he returned from the expedition and revisited Mr. Peyton's house, the latter did not recognize him at first, he had changed so much. He presented such a gaunt, haggard and worn out appearance from the excessive toil and privation he had undergone, accompanied by hunger and anxiety, that he did not look much like the stalwart individual he saw depart for the interior a month previously."

Cormack failed to meet any Beothucks, but he did make some interesting discoveries, and he did collect, as he later told the members of the Beothuck Institution, "more information concerning these people than has been obtained during the two centuries and a half in which Newfoundland has been in possession of Europeans."

Here is Cormack's brief account of his journey as he read it before a meeting of the Beothuck Institution:

Having so recently returned, I will now only lay before you a brief outline of my expedition in search of the Beothucks, or Red Indians, confining my remarks exclusively to its primary object. A

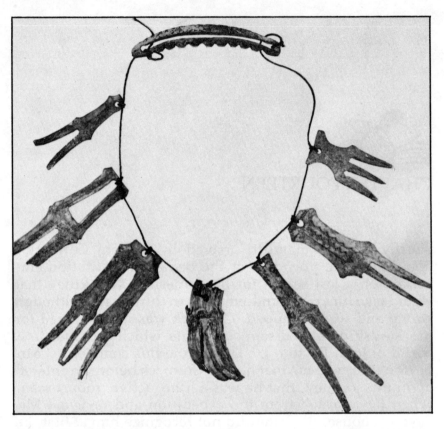

detailed report of the journey will be prepared, and submitted to
the Institution, whenever I shall have leisure to arrange the other
interesting materials which have been collected.

My party consisted of three Indians, which I procured from
among the other different tribes, viz. an intelligent and able man
of the Abenakie tribe, from Canada; an elderly Mountaineer from
Labrador; and an adventurous young Micmac, a native of this
island, together with myself. It was difficult to obtain men fit for
the purpose, and the trouble attending on this prevented my
entering upon the expedition a month earlier in the season. It was
my intention to have commenced our search at White Bay, which
is nearer the Northern extremity of the Island than where we did,
and to have travelled Southward. But the weather not permitting
to carry our party thither by water, after several days delay, I
unwillingly changed my line of route.

On the 31st of October 1828 last, we entered the country at the
mouth of the River Exploits, on the North side, at what is called the
Northern Arm. We took a Northwesterly direction to lead us to

Hall's Bay, which place we reached through an almost uninterrupted forest, over a hilly country, in eight days. This tract comprehends the country interior from New Bay, Badger Bay, Seal Bay, etc., these being minor bays, included in Green or Notre Dame Bay, at the North-east part of the island, and well known to have been always heretofore the summer residence of the Red Indians.

On the fourth day after our departure, at the East end of Badger Bay Great Lake, at a portage known as the Indian path we found traces made by Red Indians, evidently in the spring or summer of the preceding year. Their party had had two canoes; and here was a canoe-rest, on which the daubs of red-ochre, and the roots of trees used to tie it together appeared fresh. A canoe-rest is simply a few beams supported horizontally about five feet from the ground, by perpendicular posts. A party with two canoes, when descending from the interior to the sea coast, through such a part

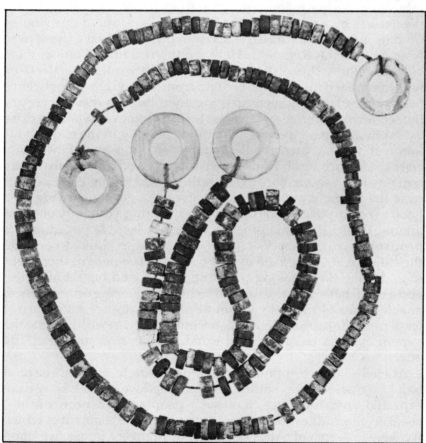

of the country as this, where there are troublesome portages, leave one canoe resting, bottom up, on this kind of frame, to protect it from injury by the weather, until their return. Among other things which lay strewed about here, were a spear shaft, eight feet in length, recently made and ochred; parts of old canoes, fragments of their skin-dresses, etc. For some distance around, the trunks of many of the birch and of that species of spruce pine called here the Var (*Pinus Balsamifera*) [sic] had been rinded; these people using the inner part of the bark of that tree for food. Some of the cuts of the trees with the axe, were evidently made the preceding year. The traces left by the Red Indians are so peculiar, that we were confident those we saw were made by them.

The spot has been a favourite place of settlement with these people. It is situated at the commencement of a portage, which forms a communication by a path between the sea-coast at Badger Bay about eight miles to the North-east, and a chain of lakes extending Westerly and Southerly from hence, and discharging themselves by a rivulet into the River Exploits, about thirty miles from its mouth. A path also leads from this place to the lakes, near New Bay, to the Eastward. Here are the remains of one of their villages, where the vestiges of eight or ten winter *mamateeks* or wigwams, each intended to contain from six to eighteen or twenty people, are distinctly seen close together. Besides these, there are the remains of summer wigwams. Every winter wigwam has close by it a small square mouthed or oblong pit, dug in the earth about four feet deep, to preserve their stores, etc. in. Some of these pits were lined with birch rind. We discovered also in this village the remains of a vapour-bath. The method used by the Beothucks to raise the steam, was by pouring water on large stones made very hot for the purpose, in the open air, by burning a quantity of wood around them; after this process, the ashes were removed, and a hemispherical framework closely covered with skins, to exclude the external air, was fixed over the stones. The patient then crept in under the skins, taking with him a birch rind bucket of water, and a small bark dish to dip it out, which by pouring on the stones, enabled him to raise the steam at pleasure. (Since my return, I learn from the captive Red Indian woman Shawnawdithit, that the vapour bath is chiefly used by old people, and for rheumatic affections.)

At Hall's Bay we got no useful information from the three (and only) English families settled there. Indeed we could hardly have expected any; for these, and such people, have been the un-checked and ruthless destroyers of the tribe, the remnant of which we were in search of. After sleeping one night at a house, we again struck into the country to the westward.

In five days we were on the highlands south of White Bay and in sight of the highlands east of the Bay of Islands, on the West coast of Newfoundland. The country south and west of us was low and flat, consisting of marshes extending in a southerly direction more than thirty miles. In this direction lies the famous Red Indians Lake. It was now near the middle of Nov. and the winter had commenced pretty severely in the interior. The country was everywhere covered with snow, and for some days past, we had walked over the small ponds on the ice. The summits of the hills on which we stood had snow on them, in some places, many feet deep. The deer were migrating from the rugged and dreary mountains in the north to the low mossy barrens, and more woody parts in the south; and we inferred, that if any of the Red Indians had been at White Bay during the past summer, they might be at that time stationed about the borders of the low tract of country before us, at the deer-passes, or were employed somewhere else in the interior, killing deer for winter provision. At these passes, which are particular places in the migration lines of path, such as the extreme ends of and straits in many of the larger lakes,—the foot of valleys between high or rugged mountains,—fords in the large rivers, and the like,—the Indians kill great numbers of deer with very little trouble, during their migrations. We looked out for two days from the summits of the hills adjacent, trying to discover the smoke from the camps of the Red Indians; but in vain. These hills command a very extensive view of the country in every direction.

We now determined to proceed towards the Red Indians' Lake sanguine that, at that known rendezvous, we would find the objects of our search.

Travelling over such a country, except when winter has fairly set in, is truly laborious.

In about ten days we got a glimpse of this beautifully majestic and splendid sheet of water. The ravages of fire, which we saw in the woods for the last two days, indicated that man had been near. We looked down on the lake, from the hills at the northern extremity, with feelings of anxiety and admiration:—No canoe could be discovered moving on its placid surface, in the distance. We were the first Europeans who had seen it in an unfrozen state, for the three former parties who had visited it before were here in the winter, when its waters were frozen and covered over with snow. They had reached it from below, by way of the River Exploits, on the ice. We approached the lake with hope and caution; but found to our mortification that the Red Indians had deserted it for some years past. My party had been so excited, so sanguine, and so determined to obtain an interview of some kind with these people, that on discovering from appearances every where around us, that the Red Indians, the terror of the Europeans as well as the other Indian inhabitants of Newfoundland,—no longer existed, the spirits of one and all of us were very deeply effected [sic]. The old Mountaineer was particularly overcome. There were everywhere indications, that this had long been the central and undisturbed rendezvous of the tribe when they had enjoyed peace and security. But these primitive people had abandoned it, after being tormented with parties of Europeans during the last 18 years. Fatal encounters had on these occasions unfortunately taken place.

We spent several melancholy days wandering on the borders of the east end of the lake, surveying the various remains of what we now contemplated to have been an unoffending and cruelly extirpated race. At several places, by the margin of the lake, small clusters of winter and summer wigwams [were] in ruins. One difference among others, between the Beothuck wigwams and those of other Indians, is, that in most of the former there are small hollows, like nests, dug in the earth around the fire place, one for each person to sit in. These hollows are generally so close together, and also so close to the fire place, and to the sides of the wigwam that I think it probable these people have been accustomed to sleep in a sitting position. There was one wooden building constructed for drying and smoking venison, in still perfect condition; also a small log house, in a dilapidated condition, which we took to have been once a store-house. The wreck of a large handsome birch rind canoe, about twenty two feet in length, comparatively new, and certainly very little used, lay thrown up among the bushes at the beach. We supposed that the violence of a storm had rent it in the way it was found and that the people who were in it had perished; for the iron nails, of which there was no want, all remained in it. Had there been any survivors, nails being much prised by those people, they never having held intercourse with Europeans, such an article would no doubt have been taken out for use again. All the birch trees in the vicinity of the lake had been rinded, and many of them and of the spruce fir or var (*Pinus balsamifera*) [sic] Canadian balsam tree, had the bark taken off, to use the inner part of it for food as noticed before.

Their wooden repositories for the dead are in the most perfect state of preservation. These are of different construction, it would appear, according to the character or rank of the person entombed. In one of them, which resembles a hut ten feet by eight or nine, and four or five feet high in the centre, floored with squared poles,

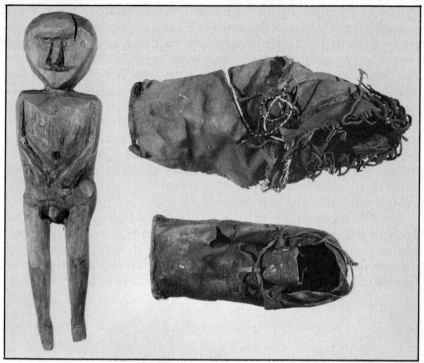

Skin moccasins and a small wooden doll found with a boy's skeleton.

the roof covered with rinds of trees, and in every way well secured against the weather inside, and the intrusion of wild beasts, there were two grown persons laid out at full length on the floor, the bodies wrapped round with deer skins. One of those bodies appeared to have been placed here not longer ago than five or six years. We thought there were children laid in here also. On first opening this building, by removing the posts which formed the end, our curiosity was raised to the highest pitch, but what added to our surprise, was the discovery of a white deal coffin, containing a skeleton neatly shrouded in muslin. After a long pause of conjecture how such a thing existed here, the idea of Mary March occurred to one of the party, and the whole mystery was at once explained. (It should be remarked here, that Mary March, so called from the name of the month in which she was taken, was the Red Indian female who was captured and carried away by force from this place by an armed party of English people, nine or ten in number, who came up here in the month of March 1819. The local government authorities at that time did not foresee the result of offering a reward to bring a Red Indian to them.)

In this cemetery were deposited a variety of articles, in some instances the property, in others the representation of the property, and utensils, and of the achievements, of the deceased. There were two small wooden images of a man and woman, no doubt meant to represent husband and wife; a small doll, which was supposed to represent a child (for Mary March had to leave her only child here, which died two days after she was taken); several small models of canoes; two small models of boats; an iron axe; a bow and quiver of arrows were placed by the side of Mary March's husband; and two fire-stones (radiated iron pyrites, from which they produced fire, by striking them together) lay at his head; there were also various kinds of culinary utensils, neatly made, of birch rind and ornamented, and many other things some of which we did not know the use or meaning.

Another mode of sepulchre which we saw here was, where the body of the deceased had been wrapped in birch rind, and with his property placed on a sort of scaffold about four feet and a half on the ground. The scaffold was formed of four posts, about seven feet high, fixed perpendicularly in the ground, to sustain a kind of

Birch bark vessels from a Beothuck child's grave.

124

crib, five feet and a half in length by four in breadth, with a floor made of small squared beams, laid close together horizontally, and on which the body and property rested.

A third mode was, when the body, bent together, and wrapped in birch rind, was enclosed in a kind of box, on the ground. The box was made of small squared posts, laid on each other horizontally, and notched at the corners to make them meet close; it was about four feet by three, and two and a half feet deep, and well lined with birch rind, to exclude the weather from the inside. The body lay on its right side.

A fourth and the most common mode of burying among these people has been to wrap the body in birch rind and cover it with a heap of stones, on the surface of the earth in some retired spot; sometimes the body, thus wrapped up, is put a foot or two under the surface, and the spot covered with stones; in one place, where the ground was sandy and soft, they appeared to have been buried deeper, and no stones placed over the graves.

These people appear to have always shewn great respect for their dead; and the most remarkable remains of them commonly observed by Europeans at the sea-coast, are their burying places. These are at particular chosen spots; and it is well known that they have been in the habit of bringing their dead from a distance to them.

On the north side of the lake, opposite the River Exploits, are the extremities of the two deer fences, about half a mile apart, where they lead to the water. It is understood that they diverge many miles in north-westerly directions. The Red Indian makes these fences to lead and scare the deer to the lake, during the periodical migration of these animals; the Indians being stationed looking out when the deer get into the water to swim across, the lake being narrow at this end, they attack and kill the animals with spears out of their canoes. In this way they secure their winter provisions before the severity of that season sets in.

There were other old remains of different kinds peculiar to these people met with about the lake.

One night we encamped on the foundation of an old Red Indian wigwam, on the extremity of a point of land which juts out into the lake, and exposed to the view of the whole country around. A large fire at night is the life and soul of such a party as ours, and when it blazed up at times, I could not help observing that two of my Indians evinced uneasiness and want of confidence in things around, as if they thought themselves usurpers on the Red Indian territory. From time immemorial none of the Indians of the other tribes had encamped near this lake fearlessly, and, as we had now done, in the very centre of such a country; the lake and territory adjacent having been always considered to belong exclusively to the Red Indians, and to have been occupied by them. It had been our invariable practice hitherto to encamp near hills, and be on their summits by dawn of day, to try to discover the morning smoke ascending from the Red Indians' camps; and to prevent the discovery of ourselves, extinguishing our own fire always some length of time before daylight.

Our only and frail hope now left of seeing the Red Indians lay on the banks of the River Exploits, on our return to the sea coast.

The Red Indians' Lake discharges itself about three or four miles from its north-east end, and its waters form the River Exploits. From the lake to the sea-coast is considered about seventy miles; and down this noble river the steady perseverance and intrepidity of my Indians carried me on rafts in four days, to accomplish which otherwise, would have required probably two weeks. We landed at various places on both banks of the river on our way down, but found no traces of the Red Indians so recent as those seen at the portage at Badger Bay, Great Lake, towards the beginning of our excursion. During our descent, we had to construct new rafts at the different water-falls. Sometimes we were carried down the rapids at the rate of ten miles an hour or more, with considerable risk of destruction to the whole party, for we were always together on one raft.

What arrests the attention most, while gliding down the stream, is the extent of the Indian fences to entrap the deer. They extend from the lake downwards, continuous, on the banks of the river at least thirty miles. There are openings left here and there in them, for the animals to go through and swim across the river, and at these places the Indians are stationed and kill them in the water with spears, out of their canoes, as at the lake. Here, then, connecting these fences with those on the north-side of the lake, is at least forty miles of country, easterly and westerly, prepared to intercept all the deer that pass that way in periodical migrations. It was melancholy to contemplate the gigantic, yet feeble efforts of a whole primitive nation, in their anxiety to provide subsistence, forsaken and going to decay.

There must have been hundreds of the Red Indians, and that not many years ago, to have kept up these fences and pounds. As their numbers were lessened so was their ability to keep them up for the purpose intended; and now the deer pass the whole line unmolested.

We infer, that the few of those people who yet survive have taken refuge in some sequestered spot, still in the northern part of

126

the island and where they can procure deer to subsist on.

On the 29th November we again returned to the mouth of the River Exploits, in thirty days after our departure from then having made a complete circuit of about 200 miles in the Red Indians territory.

At the conclusion of this speech William Cormack presented the Beothuck Institution with a variety of articles which he had collected on his journey. These included bows, arrows, spears, a model of a canoe, and a complete suit of caribou skin clothing. Regrettably, all these items have since been lost.

Cormack had another surprise for his audience. He produced a list of three hundred Beothuck words, but he did not say how he had collected these. He stated that this list "proved the Boeothicks to be a distinct tribe from any hitherto discovered in North America." Later he acknowledged that Shananditti had helped him to record the vocabulary list. (See Appendix.)

On his return in November 1828 Cormack recorded his impressions of Shananditti in his *Letter Book*: "To this interesting proteégeé we are indebted for nearly all the information we possess regarding her tribe, the aborigines of Newfoundland. Although she had been five years and upwards amongst the English, upon her arrival the second time in St. John's she spoke so little English that those only who were accustomed to her gibberish, could understand her. By persevering attention now however, to instruct her, she acquired confidence and became enabled to communicate. She evinced extraordinary powers of mind in possessing the sense of gratitude in the highest degree, strong affections for her parents and friends, and was of a most lively disposition. She had a natural talent for drawing, and being at all times supplied with paper and pencils of various colours, she was enabled to communicate what would otherwise have been lost. By this means, aided by her broken English and Beothuck words, she herself taught the meaning . . . to those around her."

Language lessons were important for the work which lay ahead and for Shananditti's adjustment to her new life in the city. Shananditti was a good student; only five weeks after her arrival in St. John's, Cormack wrote the Bishop of Nova Scotia a glowing report of her improvement:

As she acquires the English language she becomes more interesting; and I have lately discovered the key to the Mythology of her tribe, which must be considered the most interesting subjects to enquire into.

He complimented her again in a later letter to the bishop. This time he revealed how he worked with her in unlocking the secrets of her past and the mysteries of her people:

Shawnawdithit is now becoming very interesting as she improves in the English language, and gains confidence in people around. I keep her pretty busily employed in drawing historical representations of everything that suggests itself relating to her tribe, which I find is the best and readiest way of gathering information from her. She has also nearly completed making a dress of her tribe.

The collaboration of Shananditti and Cormack was one of mutual patience and gratitude, in which important information was exchanged through sympathetic comradeship. Although from widely different backgrounds, each was gentle, inquisitive, good-natured, and intelligent. And they shared a common goal: "to communicate what would otherwise have been lost."

Of the sketches which Shananditti drew for Cormack during that winter of 1828-29, only ten exist. It seems likely there were others: Cormack makes reference in his writings to notes and observations, now lost, that might have been marked on sketches.

Of the drawings that remain, five represent scenes from the closing history of Shananditti's people, and five of religion. These drawings form a unique contribution to an important and neglected period in Canadian history. Scattered across the drawings are notes in William Cormack's handwriting.

The drawings are accurate in topographical details, but they lack regular scale: rivers and lakes appear larger than they really are. Nevertheless, the details of shoreline, islands, bends in the river, falls, rapids, and junctions of rivers are accurate, and the relation of each of these to the other is correct. James Howley later remarked that "every fall, rapid and tributary or other remarkable feature is laid down, all of which I have no difficulty in recognizing from my own exploration and survey of 1875."

Without these drawings and Cormack's efforts to interpret them, the Beothucks would have remained an even more obscure and mysterious people. However, an entire culture and its customs and beliefs cannot be contained within the limits of a few drawings. And there are other problems: parts of Shananditti's drawings are difficult to interpret, and William Cormack's notes are incomplete; many have been lost.

The most striking fact depicted in these drawings is the rapid decline of the Beothuck population during Shananditti's short lifetime. William Cormack recounted that Shananditti always cried when she told him about the last days of her people. The columns of figures which he wrote on her drawings, listing the living and the dead, tragically illustrate this rapid decline. On one of her drawings Cormack noted that "The Tribe has decreased much since 1816, for it would appear that in 1820 their number only amounted to 27 in all." The information on another drawing indicates that three years later there were only twelve Beothucks left.

Shananditti knew by name all of the fifteen who perished in the winter of 1822-23, probably from starvation, a cruel death.

She told Cormack that the twelve surviving people consisted of five men, four women, one lad, and two children. He noted that: "The five men were, her uncle, two brothers of Mary March, one of whom was called Longnon, and his son. The four women were, Mary March's mother and sister, Longnon's wife and Nancy's cousin. The lad was Mary March's sister's son, and the two children, a boy and a girl, Nancy's brother's children." This is the only mention made of Shananditti's brother; presumably he had been dead for some time.

Five more Beothucks died in the spring of 1823: Shananditti's cousin, uncle, father, mother, and sister. This left seven Beothucks surviving on their own somewhere in the wilderness. All subsequent exploration failed to find any trace of them. After his final search in the fall of 1828, William

129

Cormack was forced to conclude that they had passed from existence. However, there is a persistent legend that the "final remnant" travelled safely across Newfoundland to the west coast and escaped into Labrador. There is no evidence to support this belief.

CHAPTER FIFTEEN

The ten surviving sketches by Shananditti represent an incomplete, sometimes baffling, but fascinating assortment of information. In addition to drawings of preserved food and house construction, and maps and scenes of army expeditions, captures, murders, and population decline, she made several sketches of domestic and religious life. These range from the very simple to the complex and puzzling.

The sketch of the two houses where Shananditti stayed in St. John's requires very little explanation. (See next page.) The houses are very different in size. The smaller one is identified as Roope's house. This was probably the house where Shananditti stayed with William Cormack while she was making these sketches and telling him about her people. Cormack could have rented the house from Roope. The other is large, rather stately, and not a typical colonial house. It has two stories, two front entrances, two chimneys, and eight large windows. Though not identified, it is in all likelihood the home of James Simms, the attorney general, who took an active interest in Shananditti. He took care of her after Cormack's departure for England.

More than one of Shananditti's drawings contain a number of unrelated figures and objects. (See page 133.) The person in the middle is labelled "Dancing Woman," or "Thub-wed-gie." She has long hair and her arms are uplifted in an expression of joy, but her feet seem stiffly rooted to the ground. The posture is stylized rather than realistic. The chief point of interest would appear to be her clothes. There is a decorated border at the top and bottom of her garment. It

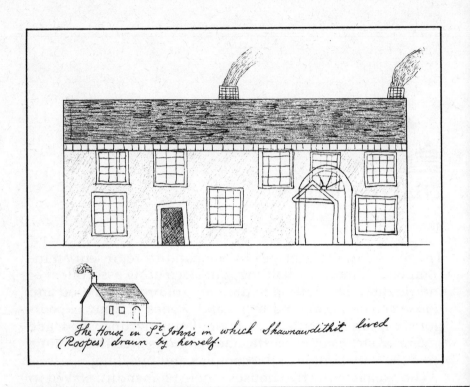

The House in St. John's in which Shawnawdithit lived (Roopes) drawn by herself.

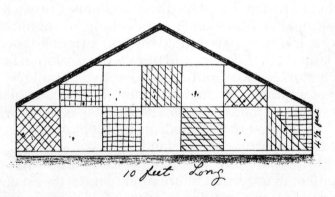

10 feet Long

Store House in which they put their dried venison, in birch rind boxes or packages to keep during Winter

132

is not possible to tell from the drawing what the border is made of, but other descriptions of Beothuck clothes state that they frequently trimmed their clothing with beaver and martin. There is a loose fringe at the bottom of her skirt which would add motion to the dance. It is difficult to know whether the garment is all of one piece or several pieces. One shoulder is bare and a portion of the garment is flying loose under the right arm. It is almost certain that it was not worn in this fashion. Shananditti probably added this to show how it was made and to indicate how it was wrapped around the body.

To the right of the dancing woman there is an assortment of birch bark containers. These include drinking cups, bowls, and water buckets. Cormack may have written a note to explain the reason for the different shapes and sizes of the water buckets. Since the buckets have two different names, they probably served different purposes.

The structure to the left of the dancing woman is labelled "Store House in which they put their dried venison in birch rind boxes or packages to keep during the winter." Only a cross-section of the building is shown, but it gives a clear

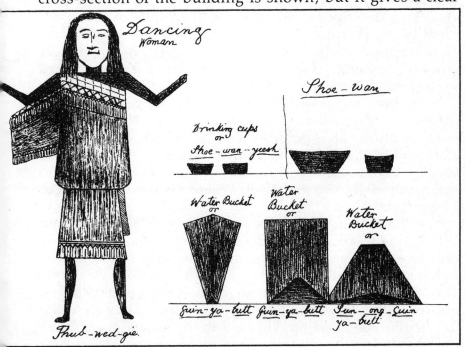

133

view of how it was used. The interior is divided into two tiers, and each is divided into squares. The shaded areas represent meat storage boxes constructed of birch bark and branches and stacked to allow open spaces between each one. The dimensions of the building are not large: it is ten feet wide and has walls four and a half feet high. (There is no indication of its length.) The roof has a low angle of slope, and it appears to be quite thick. The construction of the storehouse would have to be very strong since it would have to withstand the weight of snow and to resist the invasion of animals.

Other drawings by Shananditti are less easy to interpret. These contain enigmatic features which tease the imagination: an example in the next illustration is a strange figure of a man. One arm is raised in a gesture of greeting, and there are two curious elongated appendages hanging from his shoulders. These may be features of his clothing or physical attributes. It is difficult to tell.

A note on the drawing identifies the strange man as "Aich-mud-yim. The Black Man, or Red Indian Devil. Short and very thick; He dresses in Beaver Skin, has a long beard, etc." This description only adds to the riddle of the man's identity. Furthermore, he is not shown with a large beard. Another note reads: "Seen at Great Lake." It is not clear whether this figure is intended to represent a real person or a supernatural being.

It has been suggested that the mysterious black man is a missionary dressed in a long black loose-fitting garment with an outer cape; possibly one of the priests who were stationed at Placentia during the French occupation. This seems a bit far-fetched. How did the man of God manage to make himself known as a devil? Would a priest be dressed in beaver skins?

The black man may be a shaman, possibly of Eskimo origin. It is also possible that Shananditti never saw him but only heard stories about him, and drew him as he appeared to her imagination.

To the right of the black man are two twelve-foot spears, one for killing seals and one for killing deer. They are quite different in construction. The "a-a-duth," or seal spear, has a detachable iron head which fits into a bone socket. A long

Aich – mud – yim.

The Black man, or Red Indian's Devil.}
short & very thick; He dresses in }
Beaver Skin, }
has a large beard &c.

Seen at
the Great
Lake

ā-ā-duth, or Spear for killing Seals 12 feet long

bone iron

iron

Amuna Deer Spear

iron

135

line passes through a hole in the bone and is attached to the triangular iron head. The other end of the line is tied to a notch at the base of the spear. The head is kept in place by tension on the line, and as soon as it enters the body of the seal, it separates from the bone socket mounted on the wooden shaft. The "amina," or deer spear, has a long tapered iron head which is fitted permanently to the wooden shaft by means of a long thin stem.

Shananditti's last drawing is the most puzzling of all. It depicts a collection of six religious staves, each with a different emblem or crest. (See opposite.) When Cormack first saw these, he became quite excited and he sent a hasty note to the Bishop of Nova Scotia in which he declared, "I have lately discovered the key to the mythology of her tribe, which must be considered one of the most interesting subjects to enquire into." This section of Cormack's papers is missing.

Many people have dismissed these staves as family crests, badges of office, or simply emblems of heroic exploits such as killing a whale or stealing a fishing boat. However, such explanations may fall far short of the true significance of these staves.

The Beothuck staves were not only similar to the sun staves of ancient Egypt, but also exactly the same size. The Beothucks expanded the variety of their sun staves with such symbols as the whale's tail and the European bully boat, but the half disc of the sun, and the inverted pyramid or symbol of the sky, were the same as important Egyptian symbols.

It could be argued that the similarity between the Beothuck sun staves and the Egyptian ones is purely accidental. But contrary evidence is strong; in fact the parallels between the two cultures are astonishing.

The Beothucks worshipped the sun, and their chief deity was Kuis. The Egyptians worshipped the sun god Ra, and later Osiris. It has been suggested that the names Kuis and Osiris have a common root. This proves very little, however, since sun worship was once a world-wide religion.

The most convincing parallels are found in the Beothuck death cult and burial customs which are almost identical with those practised in Egypt. The Beothucks painted the corpse with red ochre; they buried their dead in rock tombs; the body was sometimes laid out on a table and sometimes in

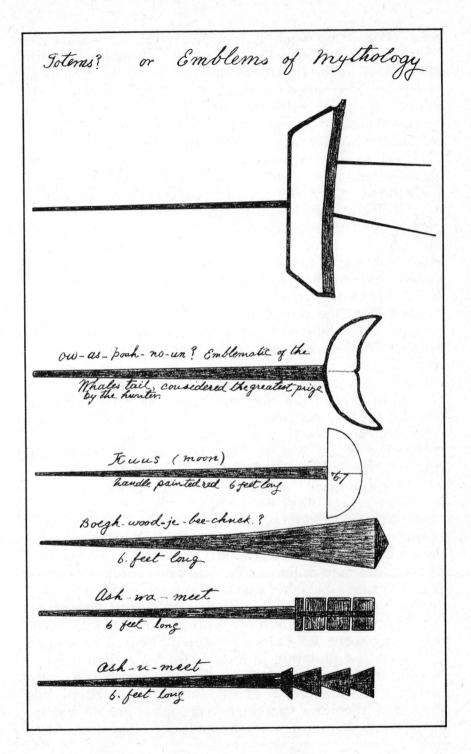

Totems?   or   Emblems of Mythology

ow-as-poah-no-un? Emblematic of the Whales tail, considered the greatest prize by the hunter.

Kuus (moon)
handle painted red 6 feet long

Boegh-wood-je-bee-chuck.?
6. feet long

Ash-wa-meet
6 feet long

Ash-u-meet
6. feet long

a flexed or sitting position; tools, weapons, food, and sacks of red ochre were buried with the body; a little boat, or ship of the dead as the Egyptians called it, was placed near the body; a small wooden image of the dead person was carved, painted with red ochre, and placed on a table beside the body. In addition, songs about death and ancestors accompanied the burial practices. Shananditti described these.

The Egyptian rites were conducted on a larger scale and embellished with greater riches, but the details are essentially the same. It is impossible to conceive that this strange death cult and complex burial ritual could have arisen independently in two separate parts of the world. Yet it is equally difficult to imagine how it was transported thousands of miles from Egypt to Newfoundland. The answer is not yet known, but one thing is certain: the array of evidence is too weighty to be dismissed as coincidence. Either one culture is derived from the other, or both sprang from a common source. When Shananditti drew the Beothuck sun staves for William Cormack, she opened the door to a fascinating mystery.

Cormack sought the answers to many questions which Shananditti could not give him. He was particularly interested in the early history of the Beothucks: where they came from and how they got to Newfoundland.

Whether North America was their original home will probably never be known for certain, but there is some evidence to suggest that they migrated from Asia across the frozen ice bridge of the Bering Strait.

The West Coast Indians, who came across the Bering Strait centuries later, shared a number of habits and customs with the Beothucks—even though the two groups were separated by four thousand miles of continent and centuries of time. The two groups used the same kind of oddly-shaped pointed paddle, the same wide bow, and the same breast ornaments. Moreover, both built dwellings with a peculiar style of sleeping arrangement: long pits were dug in the ground about a foot deep and radiating in a circle from a central fire pit. None of the many other Indian tribes between the west and east coasts of North America used this sleeping pattern. It is suggested, therefore, that the two groups of people are distant cousins, stemming from the same or related stock. Also, it is possible that this ancient race of Siberian immigrants could have inhabited most of Canada and part of the United States at one time, but they were reduced by disease, warfare, or other causes. If this is true, the Beothucks were the last survivors of an ancient Siberian race, possibly the oldest people in Canada.

CHAPTER SIXTEEN

During the six weeks that Shananditti lived in the same house with William Cormack, she was ill with tuberculosis. She never complained and was always grateful for any kindness shown her. Under Dr. Carson's care she seemed to improve gradually, and by January 1829 Cormack felt free to travel to England, leaving Shananditti comfortably housed with the family of attorney general James Simms. Before his departure Shananditti gave him a curious and touching gift which she valued greatly: two charm stones that her mother had given her. In later years Cormack discovered that these charms were identical to those used by the shamen in Tasmania. He was never able to explain this enigma.

While Shananditti stayed at the attorney general's house, a final attempt was made to convert her to Christianity. She received instruction in the Christian doctrines, but it is not clear how vigorously this was pursued. Shananditti probably viewed this as an act of kindness, but she remained faithful to her own beliefs.

Dr. Carson continued to tend Shananditti, but his medical skills could not arrest her illness. After several weeks he transferred her to the hospital. She was only twenty-eight, and death was near.

William Cormack was by then too far afield to be summoned. His successive travels took him to Australia, New Zealand, and British Columbia, where he settled in 1851 and founded an agricultural society. Throughout his life, he conducted a lively correspondence with distinguished scientists and literary figures around the world; these included Sir

William Hooker and Professor Faraday. He spent a lifetime collecting, recording and distributing information for the benefit of others.

Cormack died in New Westminster, British Columbia, in 1868. Edward Graham, a close personal friend, wrote a long obituary in the May 9 issue of the *British Columbian* which summarized his far-ranging travels and accomplishments. Graham concluded his account with these remarks:

The impulse of a strong fancy made him a wanderer—the commercial man and the explorer in one. While he sought the respectable gains of commerce, he at the same time aimed at extending international knowledge, thus contributing to the welfare and happiness of man. He was naturally of a buoyant and happy disposition, genial and kindly; his manners were suave and dignified.

Shananditti's condition grew steadily worse after Cormack's departure. Dr. Carson remained close to her, but there was very little he could do. She died in the hospital on June 6, 1829, and was buried in the Church of England Cemetery on the south side of St. John's. The record of her burial is written in the Church of England Cathedral Parish Register, and it reads as follows: "June 8th 1829. Interred Nancy, Shanawdithe aet. 23 South Side. (very probably the last of the aborigines)." It is signed by Frederick H. Carrington A.B., Rector of St. John's.

The news of Shananditti's death appeared in a St. John's newspaper on June 12:

DIED—On Saturday night the 6th inst., at the Hospital, Sha-na-dith-it, the female Indian, one of the aborigines of this Island. She died of consumption, a disease which seems to have been remarkably prevalent amongst her tribe, and which has unfortunately been fatal to all who have fallen into the hands of settlers. Since the departure of Mr. Cormack from this Island, this poor woman has had an asylum afforded her in the house of James Simms Esq., Attorney General, where every attention has been paid to her wants and comforts, and under the able and professional advice of Dr. Carson who has most liberally and kindly attended her for many months, it was hoped her health might have been re-established. Latterly however, her disease became daily more formidable, and her strength rapidly declined, and a short time since it was deemed advisable to send her to the Hospital, where her sudden decease has but too soon fulfilled the fears that were entertained of her.

Shananditti had seen her mother and sister die of the same disease; no one could hide the truth from her. She saw the approach of death and she faced it without complaint. Her short life was one of pain, suffering, and loss, yet she lived it courageously.

Shananditti's grave cannot be found in the cemetery to-day. It was dug up in later years to make way for a road. Even her bones are lost. Only her name endures. Shananditti: the last of the Beothucks.

NEWFOUNDLAND:

Some of the places mentioned in Shananditti's story

BEOTHUCK VOCABULARY

This list of Beothuck words was compiled by James Howley from four separate manuscripts. He states that "Cormack obtained his vocabulary from Shawnadithit which seems more reliable and phonetically more accurate than the one obtained from Mary March."

ABBREVIATIONS

C.—Cormack's vocabulary, from Shanawdithit.
Howl.—Corrections of Leigh's printed voc. from his own Manuscript, made by James P. Howley.
K.—Vocabulary of Dr. King, transmitted by Rob. Gordon Latham, London, April 1883.
No letter—Rev. John Leigh's voc. from Mary March (Demasduit).

VOCABULARY

A-aduth *seal-spear*, C. Cf. amina.
Abemite *gaping*.
Abideshook; Abedésoot K., *domestic cat*; cf. bidesook.
Abidish *"martin cat," marten*. Micmacs call him *cat*; the whites of
    Newfoundland call a young seal: *cat* or *harp-seal*, because a
    design visible on their backs resembles a harp[1].
Abobidress *feathers*; cf. ewinon.
Abodoneek *bonnet*, C.; abadung-eyk *hat*, K.
Adadimite or Adadimiute; andemin K. *spoon*; cf. a-enamin.
Adamadret; adamatret K. *gun, rifle*.
Adenishit *stars*; cf. shawwayet *a star*, K.
Adizabad Zea *white wife*.
Adjith *to sneeze*.
Adoltkhtek, adolthtek K., adolthe; ode-ōthyke C. *boat, vessel*
    seems to imply the idea of being pointed or curved; cf.
    A-aduth, adothook; Dhoōrado, Tapathook.
Adosook K., Aa-dāzook C. *eight*; Ee-aa-dazook *eighteen*, C.
Adothook; Adooch, K. *fish-hook*.
Aduse *leg*; ádyouth *foot*, K.
Adzeech K.; adasic; ádzeich C., *two*; ee-adzike *twelve*, C.; adzeich
    dthoónut *twenty*, C.
A-enamin *bone*, C.

A-eshemeet *lumpfish*, C.

Ae-u-eece *snail*, K.

Ae-wā-een C.; cf. ee-wa-en.

Agamet; aegumet K., *buttons; money*.

Aguathoonet *grindstone*.

Ahune, Ahunes, oun K. *rocks*. Misspelt Ahmee (Lloyd).

Ajeedick or vieedisk K. *I like*.

Akusthibit (ac- in original) *to kneel*.

Amet *awake*, C.

Amina *deer-spear*, C.

Amshut *to get up*; cf. amet. Howley supposes this to be from the same word as gamyess, q.v.

Anadrik *sore throat*; cf. tedesheet.

Anin *comet*; cf. anun *spear (in skies?)*.

Annawhadya *bread*, K.; cf. manjebathook.

Annŏŏ-ee *tree; forest, woods* K.

Ánun *spear*, C.; cf. a-duth, amina, anin, annŏŏ-ee.

Anwoyding *consort; husband*, when said by wife; *wife* when said by husband. Cf. zathrook.

Anyemen, ányēmen *bow*, K.; der. from annŏŏ-ee, q.v.

A-oseedwit *I am sleepy*, K.

Aoujet *snipe: Gallinago wilsonia*, of genus *Scolopacidae*.

Apparet o bidesook *sunken seal*.

Ardobeeshe and madobeesh *twine*, K.; cf. meroobish.

Ashaboo-uth C.; iggobauth *blood*, C.; cf. ebanthoo.

Áshautch *meat; flesh*, K.

Ashei *lean, thin; sick*.

Ashmudyim *devil*, "bad man," C.; cf. muddy. The spelling of the first syllable is doubtful.

Ashwameet, ashumeet, mythological symbol drawn by Shanaw-dithit.

Ashwan, nom. pr., *Eskimo*.

Áshwoging C.; ashoging K., *arrow*; cf. dogernat.

Asson; ásson K. *sea-gull*.

Áss-soyt *angry*, C.

Athess; áthep K. *to sit down*.

Awoodet *singing*.

Baasíck *bead*, C., bethec *necklace*.

Baasothnut; beasóthunt, beasothook K. *gunpowder*; cf. basdic.

Badisut *dancing*.

Baetha *go home*, K. becket? *where do you go?* baeōdut *out of doors*, or *to go out of doors*, K. These three words all seem to belong to the same verb.

Baroodisick *thunder*.

Basdic; basdick K. *smoke*; cf. baasothnut.

Báshedtheek; beshed K. *six*, C. Rigadosik *six* in Leigh's voc. seems to point to another dialect. Ee-beshedtheek *sixteen*, C.

Bashoodite Howl. *to bite*.

Bashubet *scratch* (verb?).

Bathuc; badoese K., watshoosooch K. *rain*; cf. ebanthoo.

Baubooshrat *fish*, K.; cf. bobboosoret *codfish*.

Bebadrook *nipper* (moskito).

Bedejamish bewajowite *May*, C.; cf. kosthabonoóng bewajowit.

Beodet *money*; cf. agamet, baasick.

Beothuk, Beothick K.; Béhat-hook K.; Boeothuck (in Howley's corresp.); Beathook. (1) *Indian*; (2) *Red Indian*, viz. Indian of Newfoundland; cf. haddabothic.

Berrooick or berroich *clouds*.

Betheoate *good night*.

Bibidegemidic *berries*; cf. manus.

Bidesook; beadzuck, bidesúk K. *seal*; cf. abideshook, apparet.

Bidisoni *sword*.

Bituwait *to lie down*.

Boad *thumb*, K.

Bobbidist Howl.; bobbodish K. *pigeon* (guillemot, a sea bird). A species of these, very abundant in Newfoundland is *Lomvia troile*[2].

Bobbiduishemet *lamp*; cf. boobeeshawt, mondicuet and emet *oil*.

Bobboosoret *codfish*; is the same word as baubooshrat.

Bogathŏowytch, *to kill*, K.; buhashauwite *to beat*; bobáthoowytch *beat him!* Beating and killing are frequently expressed by the same term in Indian languages; cf. datyuns.

Bogodoret; bedoret, bĕdoret K. *heart*.

Bogomot or bogomat *breast*, K.; boghmoot *woman's breast*, K.; bodchmoot *bosom*, C.; bemoot *breast*, C.; cf. bogodoret.

Bŏŏbasha, boobasha *warm*, K.; cf. obosheen.

Boobeeshawt *fire*, K.; cf. bobbiduishemet.

Boochauwhit *I am hungry*, K.; cf. pokoodoont.

Boodowit *duck*; cf. eesheet, mameshet.

Boos seek *blunt*, C.; pronounced búsik.

Bootzhawet *sleep* (verb?) K.; cf. isedoweet.

Botomet onthermayet; botothunet outhermayet Howl. *teeth*(?).

Boyish *birch bark*; by-yeech *birch tree*, K.

Būhāshāmēsh *white boy*, C.; buggishāmesh *boy*, K.

Buhashauwite; cf. bogathŏowytch.

Bukashaman, bookshimon *man*; buggishaman *white man*, K.

Butterweye *tea*, K. (English.)

Carmtack *to speak*, K.; ieroothack, jeroothack *speak*, K.
Cheashit *to groan*.
Cockáboset; cf. geswat.

Dábseek C., dābzeek K., abodoesic *four*; ee-dabzook *fourteen*, C.
Dattomeish; dootomeish K. *trout*.
Datyuns or datyurs *not kill*(?), K.
Dauoosett *I am hungry*, K., probably flase; cf. boochauwhit.
Debine Howl, deboin K. *egg*.
Deddoweet; didoweet K., *saw*, subst.
Deed-rashow *red*, K.
Deh-hemin Howl, dayhemin K. *give me!*
Delood! *come with us!* K. dyoom! *come hither!* K. dyoot thouret!
    come hither! C. toouet (to) *come*, K. nadyed *you come back*, K.
Demasduit, nom. pr. of *Mary March*.
Deschudodoick *to blow*, C.
Deyn-yad, pl. deyn-yadrook *bird*, C.
Dho ōrado *large boat*, K.; cf. adoltkhtek.
Dingyam, dhingyam K., thengyam *clothes*.
Dogajavick *fox*, K.; cf. deed-rashow *red*; the common fox is the red
    fox.
Dogernat *arrow*, kind of.
Doodebewshet, nom. pr. of Nancy's mother, C.
Doothun *forehead*, K.
Dósŏmite K., dosomite *pin*.
Drona; drone-ooch K. *hair*; the latter form apparently a plural.
Dthŏŏnanven, thinyun *hatchet*, K.
Dtho-ónut, C.; cf. adzeech. Dyout, dyoat, *come here*.

Ebanthoo; ebadoe K. *water*.
Ebathook *to drink*, K.; zebathŏong *to drink water*, K.; cf. ebanthoo,
    bathuc.
Edat or edot *fishing line*; cf. a-aduth, adothook.
Edrú or edree; edachoom K. *otter*.
Ee- composes the numerals of the first decad from 11 to 19; it is
    prefixed to them and emphasized; cf. the single numerals.
Eeg *fat*, adj.
Eenoaja *cold* (called?), K.
Eenódsha *to hear*, K.; cf. noduera.
Eeseeboon *cap*, K.
Eeshang eyghth *blue*, C.
Eesheet *duck*, K.; probably abbrev. of mameshet, q.v.
Eeshoo *make haste*.
Eewā-en; aewā-en K., hewhine, ŏ-ŏwin K. *knife*; cf. oun. Leigh

has also: nine, probably misspelt for: wine (wa-en).
Egibididuish, K., egibidinish *silk handkerchief*.
Ejabathook, ejabathhook K., *sail*: edjabathook sails.
Ejew *to see*, K.; pronounced idshu.
Emamoose, immămōose *woman*; emmamoose *white woman*, K.
Emamooset *child*; *girl*; emmamooset *white girl*, K.
Emet; emet K. *oil*; composes bobbiduishemet and odemet, q.v.
Emoethook; emmathook K. *dogwood* (genus: *Cornus*) or *mountain Ash*.
Ethenwit; etherwit Howl. *fork*.
Euano *to go out*; enano *go out*, Howl.
Ewinon *feather*, K.

Gaboweete *breath*, C.
Gamyess *get up*, Howl.
Gasook or yasook, yosook *dry* K.; gasuck, gassek, K. *stockings*.
Gausep *dead*, K.; gosset *death*, and *dead*, K.
Geonet *tern*, *turr*[3], a sea-swallow; Lomvia troile (also called Urea troile), K. has geonet fur.
Ge-oun K.; gown *chin*.
Geswat *fear*, K.; cockáboset! *no fear! do not be afraid!* K.
Gheegnyan, geegn- yan, K., guinya *eye*.
Gheen K., geen (or gun?) *nose*.
Gidyeathuc *wind*.
Gigarimanet K., giggeramanet; giggamahet Howl. *net*.
Gobidin *eagle*, C.
Godabonyeesh *November*, C.
Godabonyegh, *October*, C.
Godawik *shovel*; cf. hadowadet.
Gonathun- keathut Howl.; cf. keathut.
Goosheben *lead* (v. or subst.?)
Gotheyet *ticklas*[4], a bird of the genus *Sterna*; species not identifiable, perhaps *macrura*, which is frequent in Newfoundland (H. W. Henshaw)?
Gowet *scollop* or *frill*; a bivalve, *pecten*.
Guashawit *puffin*; a bird of the Alcidae family: *Lunda cirrhata*[5].
Guashuwit; gwashuwet, whashwitt, washawet K. *bear*.
Gauthin; cf. keathut.
Gungewook Howl. *mainland*.

Haddabothic *body*; hadabatheek *belly*, C.; contains beothuk, q.v.
Hádalahét K.; hadibiet *glass*; cf. nádalahet.
Hadowadet *shovel*, K.; cf. godawik.
Hanawāsutt *flatfish* or *halibut*, K.

Hanyees *finger*, K.
Haoot *the devil*, K.
Hodamishit *knee*.
Homedich, homedick, oomdzech K., *good*.

Ibadinnam *to run*, K.; cf. wothamashet.
Immămooset; cf. emamoose.
Isedoweet *to sleep;* cf. bootzhawet.
Itweena *thumb;* cf. boad.
Iwish *hammer*, K.; cf. mattuis.

Jewmetchem, jewmetcheen *soon*, K.
Jiggamint *gooseberry*.

Yaseek C., Yāzeek K., gathet *one;* ee-yaziech *eleven*, C.
Yeathun, ethath *yes*, K.
Yéothoduc *nine*, C.; ee-yéothoduck *nineteen*, C.
Yeech *short*, K.

Kaasussabook, causabow *snow*, K.
Kadimishuite *tickle;* a rapid current where the tide ebbs and flows
    in a narrow channel of the sea.
Kaesinguinyeet *blind*, C.; from gasook *dry*, gheenyan *eye*.
Kannabuch *long*, K.
Kawingjemeesh *shake hands*, K.
Keathut, gonathun- keathut; ge-outhuk K., guathin; *head*.
    Keoosock., kaasook *hill*, K.
Kewis, Kuis, ewis, keeose K. *sun; moon; watch*. Kuis *halfmoon;* a
    mythological symbol drawn by Shanawdithit.
Kingiabit *to stand*.
Kobshuneesamut (ee accented) *January*, C.
Koshet *to fall*.
Kosthabonóng bewajowit *February*, C. For the last part of word, cf.
    bedejamish bewajowite.
Kōsweet K., osweet *deer* (caribou).
Kowayaseek *July*, C.; contains yazeek *one*.
Kusebeet *louse*.

Lathun; lathum (?) *trap*, K.; cf. shabathoobet.

Madabooch *milk*, K.
Máduck, Máduch *to-morrow*, K.
Madyrut *hiccough*.
Maemed, maelmēd; mewet *hand*, K.; cf. meesh in kawingjemeesh;

meeman monasthus *to shake hands.* Memayet *arms.*

Magaraguis, magĕragueis *son,* K.

Magorun; magorum K. *deer's horns.*

Mamashee K.; mamzhing *ship, vessel.*

Mamatrabet a long (illegible; *song?*) K.

Mamashet; memeshet Howl., *ducks and drakes* (drake: male duck) probably the mallard duck, *Anas boschas*[6].

Mameshook, mamudthun K. *mouth;* cf. memasook.

Mammateek, cf. meotick.

Mamishet, Māmset, mamseet K., mámisut C. *alive.* Doodebewshet mamishet gayzoot, or D. mamisheet gayzhoot, *Doodebewshet is alive,* K. mamset *life,* K.

Mamjaesdoo, nom. pr. of Nancy's father.

Mammadronit (or -nut) *lord bird,* or *harlequin duck,* contains drona.

Mammasheek *islands;* cf. mamashee.

Māmmăsăveet (or māmmŏosĕrnit J. Peyton), mamasămeet K., mámudthuk, mamadthut K. *dog,* Māmmusemītch, pl. mammasavit *puppy.*

Mamshet, maumsheet K. *beaver* (simply: animal).

Manaboret K., manovoonit Howl. *blanket.*

Manamiss *March, month of,* C.

Mandeweech, maudweech *bushes,* K.

Mandzey, mamdsei K., mandzyke C. *black.*

Manjebathook *bread,* C.

Manegemethon *shoulder.*

Mangaroonish or mangaroouish *sun;* probably *son;* cf. magaraguis.

Manune *pitcher, cup.*

Manus *berries,* K.; cf. bibidegemidic.

Marmeuk *eyebrow.*

Mārot *to smell,* K. (v. intr.?).

Mássooch, másooch *salt water,* K.

Matheoduc *to cry.*

Mathik, mattic *stinking:* mattic bidesuk *stinking, rotten seal*[7], K.: mathic bidesook *stinking seal;* cf. mārot.

Mattuis Howl. *hammer;* cf. iwish.

Memasook, mamudth-uk, mamadth-ut K. *tongue;* cf. mameshook.

Mamayet *arms;* cf. maemed.

Meotick, meeootick, mae-adthike K. *house, wigwam.* Mammatik *house,* mammateek Howl. *winter wigwam,* meothick *house, hut, tilt camp,* K. (probably a windbreak).

Meroobish *thread;* cf. ardobeeshe.

Messiliget-hook *baby,* K.

Methabeet *cattle*, K.; nethabete *"cows and horses."*

Miaoth, *to fly*.

Modthamook *sinew of deer*, K.

Moeshwadit *drawing (?)*, mohashaudet or meheshaudet *drawing-knife* K.

Moidensu *comb*.

Moisamadrook *wolf*.

Mokothut, species of a blunt-nosed *fish*, C.

Monasthus *(to touch?)*, meeman monasthus *to shake hands*; cf. maemed.

Mondicuet *lamp*, K.; cf. bobbiduishemet.

Moocus *elbow*.

Moomesdick, nom. pr. of Nancy's grandfather.

Mooshaman, mootdhiman K. *ear*.

Mŏosin *moccasin*, K., mosen *shoe*, K.

Moosindgei- jebursūt *ankle*, C., contains mŏosin.

Mossessdeesh; cf. mozazeosh.

Motheryet *cream jug*; cf. nádalahet.

Mowageenite *iron*.

Mowead *trousers*, K.

Mozazeosh, mogazeesh K. *Red Indian boy*, mossessdeesh *Indian boy*, C.

Muddy, mandee K., múd'ti C. *bad, dirty*, mūdeet *bad man*, C.; cf. eshmudyim.

Nádalahet *cream-jug*; cf. hádalahét, motheryet.

Nechwa *tobacco*, K., deh- hemin neechon! *give me tobacco!* Howl.

Newin, newim *no*, K.

Ninezeek C., nunyetheek K., nijeek, nijeck, *five*, ee-ninezeek *fifteen*, C.

Noduera *to hear*, K.; cf. eenódsha.

Nonosabasut, nom. pr. of Demasduit's husband; tall 6 feet 7½ inches.

Oadjameet C. *to boil*, as water; v. trans. or intr.? moodamutt *to boil*, v. trans. C.

Obosheen *warming yourself*; cf. bŏŏbasha.

Obsedeek *gloves*, K.

Obseet *little bird* (species of?), C.

Odasweeteeshamut *December*, D.; cf. odusweet.

Odemen, ode- emin K., odemet *ochre*; cf. emet.

Odensook; odizeet, odo-ezheet K. *goose*; cf. eesheet *duck*.

Odishuik *to cut*.

Odjet *lobster*, K. and Leigh.

154

Odoit *to eat*; cf. pokoodoont.

Odusweet, eduswee̠t K. *hare*; cf. kosweet, odasweeteeshamut.

Oŏdrat K., woodrut *fire*; cf. boobeeshawt.

O-odosook, oodzook C., ode-ŏzook K. *seven*, ee-oodzook *seventeen*, C.

Ooish *lip*.

Oosuck *wife*; cf. woas-sut.

Osavate *to row*; cf. wotha-in, wothamashet.

Oseenyet K., ozegeen Howl. *scissors*.

Osthuk *tinker* (J. Peyton); also called guillemot, a sea bird of the genus Urea[8]. Species not identifiable.

Oun; cf. ahune.

Owasboshno-un(?) C. *whale's tail*, a mythological emblem drawn by Shanawdithit; Dr Dawson thinks it is a totem.

Ozeru, ozrook K. *ice*.

Podibeak, podybear Howl. *oar, paddle*; cf. osavate.

Pokoodoont, pokoodsont, bococtyone *to eat*, K.; cf. odoit.

Poochauwhat *to go to bed*, K.; cf. a-oseedwit.

Pugathoite *to throw*.

Quadranuek, quadranuk K. *gimlet*.

Quish *nails*.

Shabathoobet Howl., shabathootet *trap*.

Shamoth, thámook, shamook, shāamoc K. *capelan*, a fish species[9].

Shanandithit C., Shanawdithit, nom. pr. of Nancy, a Beothuc woman.

Shanung, Shŏnack, Shawnuk, Shannok, nom. pr., *Micmac Indian*, Shonack "bad Indians," *Micmacs*; cf. Sho-udamunk.

Shápoth K., shaboth *candle*.

Shánsee C. and K., theant *ten*.

Shawatharott, Shawdthārut, nom. pr., *Red Indian man*; cf. zathrook.

Shawwayet *a star*; cf. àdenishit.

Shebohoweet K., shebohowit, sheebuint C. *woodpecker*.

Shebon, sheebin *river, brook*, K.

Shedbasing wáthik *upper arm*, C.

Shedothun, shedothoon *sugar*, K.

Sheedeneesheet *cocklebur*, K.

Shegamite *to blow the nose*.

Shema bogosthuc *muskito*; cf. bedadrook.

Shendeek C., shendee K., thedsic *three*, ee-shendeek *thirteen*, shendeek dthō-ōnut *thirty*, C.

Shewthake *grinding stone*, K.; cf. aguathoonet.
Shoe-wana, shuwān *water bucket*, of birch bark, *drinking cup*, K.,
shoe-wan-yeesh *small stone vessel*, C. A drawing of a shuwan,
made by Shanawdithit, has been preserved (Howley).
Shō-udamunk (from Peyton), nom. pr. of the Mountaineer (or
Algonkin) Indians of Labrador, *Naskapi*, or "good Indians";
cf. Shanung.
Sosheet *bat*, K.
Shucododimet K., shucodimit, a plant called *Indian cup*[10].

Tapathook, dapathook K. *canoe*; cf. adoltkhtek.
Tedesheet *neck, throat*.
Theehone *heaven*, K.
Thengyam *clothes*; cf. dingyam.
Thine *I thank you*.
Thooret *come hither!* abbrev. from the full dyoot thouret C.; cf.
deiood!
Thoowidgee *to swim*.
Toouet; cf. deiood!

Wabee *wet*, K.; probably misunderstood for *white*.
Wadawhegh *August*, C.
Wāsemook *salmon*, K.; cf. wothamashet.
Washa-geuis K., washewnish *moon*.
Wāshāwet, whashwitt K.; cf. guashuwit.
Washewtch K., washeu *night, darkness*; cf. month's names.
Washoodiet, wadshŏŏdet *to shoot*, K.
Wasumaweeseek *April, June, September*, C. Said to mean "first
sunny month"; cf. wāsemook.
Watshoosooch *rain*, K.; cf. bathic.
Wáthik *arm*, C., wātheēkee *the whole arm*, K.; cf. shedbasing.
Waunathoake, nom. pr. of Mary March (Howley).
Wawashemet ŏ-ŏwin mŏŏ meshduck *we give you* (thee) *a knife*, K.
Weenoun *cheek*, K.; cf. ge-oun.
Weshomesh (Lloyd, washemesh) *herring*; cf. wothamashet. Mr
Howley thinks that Washimish, the name of an Island, con-
tains this term.
Whadicheme; cf. bogathŏowytch *to kill(?)*.
Widumite *to kiss*.
Woadthoowin, woad-hoowin *spider*, K.
Woas-eeash, woas-eesh *Red Indian girl*, K.
Woas-sut *Red Indian woman*, K., same as oosuck.
Wobee *white*, K.; cf. wabee.
Wobesheet *sleeve*, K.

Woin Howl., waine *hoop*.
Woodch *blackbird*[11], C.
Woodum *pond*, K.
Wothamashet Lloyd, *to run*, woothyat *to walk*.

Zathrook *husband*; cf. anwoyding.
Zeek *necklace*, K., abbr. from baasick (?).
Zósoot K., Zosweet *partridge*. Ptarmigan is added to the term; but a ptarmigan (Lagopus alba) is not a partridge[12].

BEOTHUCK SONG PRESERVED BY CORMACK.

Subjects of:—Bafu Buth Baonosheen Babashot, Siethodaban-yish, Edabansee,—Dosadōŏosh,—Edabanseek.

NOTES

1 This so-called harp does not develop till the animal attains its third year.
2 Sea pigeon, Black guillemot, *Uria grylle*.
3 Two entirely different species of birds. The tern is, *Sterna Wilsoni*. The Turr is, *Urea arra* or *lomvia*.
4 Kittiwake Gull, *Rissa tridactylus*.
5 *Fraturcula arctica*.
6 More probably the eider duck, *Somateria mollissima*.
7 Perhaps, *Phoca foetida*.
8 Thick billed Guillemot, *Alca torda*.
9 *Mallotus villosus*.
10 *Sarracenia purpurea*.
11 Robin thrush, *Turdus migratorius*, called Blackbird in Newfoundland.
12 The Willow grouse, always called partridge, locally.

BIBLIOGRAPHY

Blake, E. "The Beothuks of Newfoundland." *Nineteenth Century*, XXIV (1888), 889-918.

Burrage, H.S., ed. *Early English and French Voyages*. New York, 1906. Pp. 4-24.

Busk, G. "Description of Two Beothuc Skulls," *JAI*, V (1875), 230-32.

Chamberlain, A.F. "The Beothuks of Newfoundland," *AAR* (1905), 117-22.

Chappell, E. *Voyage of His Majesty's Ship* Rosemond *to Newfoundland*. London, 1818. Pp. 69-87.

Gatschet, A.S. "The Beothuk Indians," *PAPs* (1885-90), XXII, 408-24; XXIII, 411-32; XXVIII, 1-16.

Harp, E. "An Archaeological Survey in the Strait of Belle Isle Area," *AAn*, XVII (1951), 203-20.

Hewitt, J.N.B. and Gatschet, A.S. "Beothukan Family," *BBAE*, XXX, i (1907), 141-42.

Howley, J.P. *The Beothucks or Red Indians*. Cambridge, 1915.

Jenness, D. "Notes on the Beothuk Indians of Newfoundland," *BCDM*, LVI (1929), 36-37.

Klittke, M. "Die Beothuk-Indianer von Neufundland," *Aus Allen Weltheilen*, XXV (1894), 235-47.

Lloyd, T.G.B. "A Further Account of the Beothucs of Newfoundland," *JAI*, V (1875), 222-30.

———. "On the 'Beothucs,' " *JAI*, IV (1874), 21-39.

———. "On the Stone Implements of Newfoundland," *JAI*, V (1875), 233-48.

Macdougall, A. "The Boeothic Indians," *TCI*, II (1891), 98-102.

Morice, A.G. "Disparus et survivants," *BSGQ*, XX (1926), 78-94.

Murray, C.A. *The Red Indians of Newfoundland*. Philadelphia, 1854.

Patterson, G. "Beothik Vocabularies," *PTRSC*, X, ii (1892), 19-32.

———. "The Beothiks or Red Indians of Newfoundland," *PTRSC*, IX, ii (1891), 123-71.

Pilot, W., and Gray, L.H. "Beothuks," *ERE*, II (1910), 501-3.

Ryan, D.W.S. "Relics of a Lost Race," *Atlantic Guardian*, V (1948), 41-44.

Speck, F.G. "Beothuk and Micmac," *INM*, ser. 2, XXII (1921), 1-187.

———. "The Beothuks of Newfoundland," *SW*, XLI (1913), 559-63.

———. "Eskimo Jacket Ornaments of Ivory suggesting Function of Bone Pendants Found in Beothuk Sites in Newfoundland," *Aan*, V (1940), 225-28.

Townsend, C.W., ed. *Captain Cartwright and His Labrador Journal*. Boston, 1911. Pp. 16-25.

Willoughby, C.C. *Antiquities of the New England Indians*. Cambridge, 1935. Pp. 11-15.

Wintemberg, W.J. "Shell Beads of the Beothuk Indians," *PTRSC*, ser. 2, XXX, ii (1936), 23-26.